T0269942

It's Not Banter, It's Racism

It's Not Banter, It's Racism

What Cricket's Dirty Secret Reveals about Our Society

Azeem Rafiq

First published in Great Britain in 2024 by Trapeze
an imprint of The Orion Publishing Group Ltd
Carmelite House, 50 Victoria Embankment
London EC4Y 0DZ

An Hachette UK Company

1 3 5 7 9 10 8 6 4 2

Copyright © Azeem Rafiq 2024
Foreword © Jonathan Liew 2024

The moral right of Azeem Rafiq to be identified as
the author of this work has been asserted in accordance
with the Copyright, Designs and Patents Act of 1988.

All rights reserved. No part of this publication may be
reproduced, stored in a retrieval system, or transmitted
in any form or by any means, electronic, mechanical,
photocopying, recording, or otherwise, without the
prior permission of both the copyright owner and the
above publisher of this book.

A CIP catalogue record for this book is
available from the British Library.

ISBN (Hardback) 978 1 3987 1240 9
ISBN (Export Trade Paperback) 978 1 3987 1241 6
ISBN (eBook) 978 1 3987 1243 0
ISBN (Audio) 978 1 3987 1244 7

Typeset by Born Group
Printed and bound in Great Britain by Clays Ltd, Elcograf S.p.A.

www.orionbooks.co.uk

This book is dedicated to . . .

My oldest child Alyaan, who gave me the inspiration to
start this campaign . . .
My other children, Ayaan and Mirha, who gave me the
motivation to keep going . . .
And Faryal, who lived every second of the struggle and
supported me every step of the way.
To my parents, Rafiq and Rehana, who moved from
Pakistan to protect me, stayed in England to encourage
me and left England to support me. You instilled the
values I have tried to uphold.
And to my siblings and their partners, Annie, Khurrum,
Danial, Rachel, Amna, Rahila and Usman.
I know this struggle has caused a lot of discomfort to all
of you. I thank you for your support.
I hope I have made you proud and I hope your
children are only ever known by the names you give
them.

Contents

Foreword by Jonathan Liew

Media is by its very nature irrevocably drawn to novelty and impact, shock value and freshness. Outcomes rather than processes. Events rather than evolution. By way of example, one of the reasons it took societies so long to inform themselves adequately about the dangers of climate change is that for the most part climate change is the sort of thing that is constantly happening without ever really seeming to happen at all. There was no great step change, no single cataclysmic event upon which you might justifiably lead a news bulletin. Just a long and foreboding slide towards oblivion. 'Breaking: Planet Still Approaching Catastrophe, Albeit Very Slowly!' lacks a certain, you know, pizzazz.

And so for all the things the media does very well – capturing attention, generating debate, telling you exactly what a thing is, what time it starts and what channel you can watch it on – there are also things it does extremely badly. The harsh light of scrutiny can identify and condemn problems without ever coming close to providing solutions. The sequestered impregnability of most media outlets allows them to impugn and accuse without ever being required to provide a human face of their own or hold themselves to account. The editors and proprietors of newspapers and news websites are not elected, not subject to freedom of information or transparency laws, are under no obligation whatsoever to speak to the public, justify themselves or face questions, identify their motivations or their sources of funding. These are essentially floating orbs in the ether: businesses who are allowed to tell people how to think without ever showing their working.

There is, perhaps, a certain sour irony in the fact that the same currents and characteristics that allowed Azeem Rafiq to be heard also allowed him to be misheard. The same outlets that gave him hope also betrayed and crushed that hope. The same media apparatus that allowed him to tell his story in the first place also ended up traducing and distorting that story. And in the end, it was a story that ended largely in the same place it began: with the old guard back in charge at Yorkshire, with the systems and structures that enabled his treatment left largely untouched, and with Azeem himself on the outside, waving his arms and sounding warnings, talking to a public that on many levels had simply ceased to listen.

In order to explain how it all happened, we probably need to establish a few home truths first. 'The media' is, of course, not one thing but a whole ecosystem of thrashing organisms, operating across a multitude of platforms and talking across a multitude of spaces. Tabloid newspapers and broadsheet newspapers; radio and television and their various digital inheritors; websites and magazines. This is largely why it's such a hard phenomenon to pin down. Pick virtually any topic across the entirety of humanity – the war in Gaza, the new Olivia Rodrigo album, the potholes at the end of your road – and you can pretty much guarantee that somebody in the media will be doing good work on it, and somebody in the media will be spouting arrant nonsense about that exact same thing. Indeed in the age of the algorithmic news feed, your concept of what 'the media' is will be entirely unique to you alone. And so politicians and public relations experts like to talk about 'cut-through': the story or issue that can rise above the blizzard of scrolling updates and real-time takes and fractured subjectivities, and become – however fleetingly – the Thing That People Are Talking About. For a couple of weeks in late 2021, maybe a little less, that thing was Azeem Rafiq.

Why did it take so long for this story to become a story? And why did it blow up so big when it did? It was back in the thwarted lockdown months of 2020 that Azeem first gave an interview to the *Wisden* journalist Taha Hashim. Ostensibly, the interview was about his provision of free meals for key workers during the pandemic. But as we now know, the conversation went into much broader areas. Azeem spoke about the racism he had experienced at Yorkshire, an 'openly racist' captain, a dressing room in which racist comments were regarded as humorous, a culture in which complaints about racism were either ignored or turned against him. The piece was shared a little, discussed a little. But given *Wisden*'s relatively small cultural and social media footprint, it was never going to go much further than that. Weeks later, when further accusations were made by Azeem in an interview with the far larger ESPNcricinfo website, Yorkshire launched an internal inquiry possibly with the hope of kicking the issue into the long, forgotten grass.

Which is basically what happens to most things, most of the time. And be warned: this is as much your fault as it is ours in the media. Attention spans are short, and airtime and column inches are limited, and media organisations are operating in a precarious and competitive environment, and nobody reads everything, and so most things of note that happen anywhere in the world either go unreported, or reported so lightly that the vast majority of people never notice. Azeem's claims barely appeared in the national press at all for about a year. All that changed over the course of a tumultuous few weeks in November 2021.

Perhaps the most significant catalyst was the widely shared revelation by George Dobell in ESPNcricinfo that Yorkshire's internal investigation into the affair had concluded that the repeated use of 'Paki' was 'in the spirit of friendly banter'. And really for a thirsty news media there were three irresistible ingredients here. Firstly, the emotive dimension: the very fact of racist bullying, the clear injustice, the institutional incompetence. Secondly, the speed of the reaction: the real-time condemnations from senior political figures like Health Secretary Sajid Javid, the flight of sponsors and partners, the ECB's decision to strip Yorkshire of international hosting rights. Thirdly, there was the sense of unsolved mystery. The redactions in the leaked report created unnamed villains who needed to be exposed and unmasked, albeit after a sufficiently feverish period of baseless speculation and rumour. The Yorkshire racism story was a farce, a fast-moving scandal and a whodunnit all in one. One new, two news, the news.

The next significant milestone was Azeem's attendance at an evidence session at the Culture, Media and Sport parliamentary committee. For the first time, television broadcasters had a visual element to illustrate their coverage, which to this point had consisted almost entirely of talking heads, written statements rendered on a coloured text box, and beleaguered men walking down a street pursued by microphones. Perhaps we forget the importance of aesthetic in rendering stories newsworthy in the eyes of the media. Aesthetic is why broadcasters love wars and natural disasters. Aesthetic is why Donald Trump's political career managed to gain such momentum in such a short space of time. And so now, finally, the decades-long scandal of institutional racism in English cricket had a face, a name, and a set of legible human emotions.

The initial coverage of the parliamentary hearing was a mixture of shock and snowballing outrage. The prime minister Boris Johnson was forced to comment. The BBC's political show *Question Time* debated whether the word 'Paki' was racist or not. But for the most part the reaction to Azeem's case, even in outlets that would later become overtly hostile to his version of events, was sympathetic. 'Azeem Rafiq, the voice of the voiceless, has been heard,' wrote Michael Atherton in *The Times*. 'Now cricket must listen.'

But then, as is always the case with such stories, everyone moved on. Essentially, the news agenda is a child. It gets distracted by shiny things. It wails incoherently for attention. Above all it gets bored easily and struggles to focus on any single thing for more than a few days. And so once the initial shock value of Azeem's testimony had subsided, so did the mainstream coverage. Before long the only outlets still reporting the story were the dedicated cricket journalists, writing for a dedicated cricket audience, many of them quietly outraged at what this delinquent troublemaker had done to their safe, white, peaceful, conservative sport. The fact that Azeem was seeking not to centre his own story but to open a wider discussion about endemic structural racism was largely ignored. Human faces can tell a story better than any volume of data or empirical research. Initially Azeem's plight, and his skill in narrating it, helped the issue gain traction. But it also meant that when the inevitable backlash occurred, he would become its lightning rod.

Even though Azeem made it clear from the start of the process that he was not interested in claiming scalps, so much of the media's energy was nevertheless trained in this direction:

5

who might resign next, who said what to whom. Personalities sell. Anger sells. Dispute, debate, disagreement, the deliberate stirring of emotions. That which is dignified must be made profane. That which is profane must be dignified. Where do you go from 'this is racist'? Well, if you are the right-wing press, the logical next step is to volte-face, and declare that the thing everyone once agreed was racist is – in fact – not racist at all.

At which point I probably need to declare something of an interest. I joined the *Telegraph* in 2008, straight out of university. I worked there for nine years, enjoyed pretty much all of them, but let's just say things changed pretty substantially over the time I was there. The *Telegraph* has always been a conservative newspaper, but for most of its history it had a reputation for fairness and standards. The news was the news, and the comment pages were the comment pages. Truth was objective, and still an objective worth pursuing. Progressive voices, even Labour voices, were always incorporated for balance. Many of my colleagues were left-wing, and of course on the sport desk we were largely immune from the politics of the newspaper at large.

It's hard to say exactly when things started to change. But the forces driving that change were clear enough. Let's just imagine, for the sake of argument, that you're running a newspaper in the pre-internet age. You feel like you've got a decent idea of who your readers are, what they think, where they live. You can see where your newspapers are being bought, and the circulation numbers will tell you how popular you are overall, and of course a small fraction of your audience will write in to send direct feedback. But these are extremely blunt tools, almost a kind of guesswork. You can't ever really be sure who is reading your paper or why. But then, from around the turn of the century, online changes the game. Advances in technology and data capture allow you to see – for the first time – who's reading, exactly what articles they're reading, and how long they're reading for. This was the dawning of the age of the algorithm. And at the *Telegraph*, the algorithm was telling us exactly where to focus our attentions.

The problem with the algorithm is that it never knows when to push back on itself. Watch one YouTube video on how to change a car battery, and long after you have restarted your car, the site will continue to feed you car-battery videos, having identified you as some onanistic lead-acid fiend. Search the web for your next holiday and you will still be getting adverts for flights and car hire long after your tan has faded. None of this, in itself, is necessarily harmful or pernicious. But when applied to the media, and particularly politics, it creates a vicious doom-spiral that goes a long way to explaining not just the persecution of Azeem, but plenty else about our current political moment.

And so began media's long slide rightwards: towards the embrace of far-right voices and extremist views, climate sceptics and vaccine sceptics, writers and ideas that would once have been deemed beyond the pale. In the below-the-line reader comments section, there are commenters who actively deride the Conservative Party under Boris Johnson and Rishi Sunak – two of the most right-wing prime ministers in recent British history – as somehow insufficiently conservative, even traitors to the cause in comparison to true believers. There is a world-view here, and it shares many of the characteristics of nascent fascism: a grotesque obsession with race and racial purity, a demand not just for borders to be tightened but to be closed altogether, and above all an unquenchable desire to stamp on perceived enemies, be they 'globalists', 'cultural Marxists', the woke, the young, trans people, queer people, people of colour, Muslims, or indeed anybody who does not share their shrinking and sinister paranoia. For decades the press – and indeed society at large – had largely succeeded in marginalising these ideas and these people to the fringes of mainstream debate. Now, all of a sudden, they were at the wheel.

Even so, the link between what the readers want and what gets published is never quite as directly causal as people imagine. Because there is of course a layer of mediation here: the editorial department, comprised overwhelmingly of white men of middle age and comfortable means, who owe their jobs and their status to the patronage of the opaque billionaires who bankroll the entire enterprise. Rupert Murdoch: the *Sun*, *The Times* and the *Sunday Times*. Lord Rothermere: the *Daily Mail*, the *Mail on Sunday*, the *i* and the *Evening Standard*. The Barclay Brothers: until recently the owners of the *Daily* and *Sunday Telegraph*. What does all that wealth and privilege get you? It buys you a platform and a mouthpiece to expound and expand upon your own particular view of the world, your own priorities, your own battles and beefs. It buys you expensive lawyers who can firewall you against the courts. It buys influential columnists and writers, and the audiences they command.

The media platformed a deluge of negative stories that would assail Azeem over the coming weeks and months. Historic anti-Semitic comments. Accusations of sexual harassment, homophobia, misuse of Sport England money, gambling debts, partying, drinking. The public interest justification for these stories was next to zero, even before you took into account the specious and poorly sourced nature of the reporting itself. But if you're a national newspaper editor, working fourteen-hour days in a windowless office, doing some billionaire's grubby bidding while your kids get tucked into bed by somebody else, there is a kind of vicarious thrill in slashing down a sacred cow, in hunting and maiming for sport, in getting blind drunk on what dwindling power you have to make misery of human lives. I suppose the point here is that readers of the *Telegraph* – or indeed the *Mail* or the *Yorkshire Post* – were not, initially, demanding en masse that Rafiq be brought down. But what demand there was could easily be nurtured and fuelled, each hit piece creating the emotional momentum that would justify the next. The more fun it became, the more self-righteous they felt. And the more self-righteous they felt, the more fun the next attack would be.

And of course the targeting of Azeem was by no means the first, or even the worst. Once the right-wing press decides that a target is fair game, they will stop at virtually nothing in their pursuit. Princess Diana found that out, as did Meghan Markle after her, as did Gary Lineker and Marcus Rashford and Raheem Sterling and a thousand other public figures who ended up as pieces in somebody else's game. For his part, Azeem had no column in the *Daily Telegraph* or *The Times*. He had no battery of well-paid investigative reporters on the payroll. Indeed it was no coincidence that so many of the journalists now going after him were from a very different demographic to his, with stronger links to the cricketing estab-lishment, with more sources in positions of power.

And so, when they come under siege, the same institutions that shelter institutional racism shelter themselves. While the victims of the structure struggle for an audience who will listen to their stories, wait patiently for people to notice, those with a platform and the patronage of the powerful get unlimited latitude to make their case, to smear their enemies, to establish their own interpretation of the facts. There was an opportunity here, fleeting though it was, for English cricket to be remade for the better, for its structures to be refitted, for its culture to be rewired. But instead of exploring Azeem's claims more thoroughly, it closed ranks, retreated into the more familiar territory of deflection and debate, conflict and vindictiveness, recrimination and revenge. Azeem's first legacy – a legacy carved at great personal expense – was to expose how cricket works. His second gift may be to expose how this country works, too.

February 2024

PROLOGUE
Looking Back (2023)

When I spoke out in August 2020 about the racism I experienced at Yorkshire County Cricket Club, it was a long time coming. I'd held so much inside for so long, not least the terrible impact of losing my son Alyaan in 2018, a moment that changed my life and became a driving factor in my mission to make things better for future generations. After speaking in front of the Department for Culture, Media and Sport (DCMS) select committee in November 2021, I slept well for the first time in years. But even though I wouldn't change the decision to come forward, the time since has been filled with challenges, both practical and emotional, and the whole affair has taken a lot out of me. It has touched every aspect of my life: my family, my health, my work. And it has been extremely tough for those who have supported me as well.

The cost of becoming a whistle-blower has been high. I've lost a number of meaningful relationships as a result of speaking out. Even though I've pretended I'm OK and tried to just brush myself off and carry on, because I've always known that when you stand up for something, there are those who won't stand with you. Ultimately, if I've lost people along the way because they were uncomfortable about me standing up against racism, then that's on them, not me.

Being forced to leave the country I have always called home in 2022 was another cost of standing up for what's right. The challenges that came with speaking out – the legal process, the media attention, being in the public eye, the abuse – were not something I was prepared for. At times, I was in a really dark place. I was interviewed by Sky News and talked about how close I had come to taking my own life, so what I've had to endure over the last few years has been pretty tough to take. It's therefore taken a lot of work to get to the point that I feel a sense of pride in what I've achieved. The tolls have been serious and life-altering, and still I feel fortunate, and I hope in telling my story I can help all those out there who have suffered from abuse or racism, and continue to suffer.

The backlash for speaking out and the subsequent abuse I received, such that I had no choice but to eventually move countries, might not sound like the sort of thing that would make someone say they feel lucky – but I do. I feel incredibly lucky to have had the opportunity to have my faith slightly restored in human beings through the most incredible profes-sional and personal support I have received, which went above and beyond. Some people have contacted me in the same pain that I have experienced, struggling to get the support they need. I am lucky and grateful I've had it in abundance and pro bono, thanks to my lawyers Sonia Campbell and Harry Eccles-Williams at Mishcon de Reya, my barristers Jennifer Robinson, Paras Gorasia, Margherita Cornaglia and Nick De Marco, and Mark Leftly and the team at Powerscourt, who helped me with all communications. This professional support has been second to none, but the emotional support they pro-vided has been even more significant. I was a broken person looking for help and they rallied around in a way I could never have expected or imagined.

IT'S NOT BANTER, IT'S RACISM

Despite feeling good about where I have made it to today, considering everything I've overcome, it's important for me to live in reality. I realise racism and Islamophobia are still alive and thriving, and the challenges that I have faced are still taking place across cricket and beyond. I know there are still attempts to silence me and block the work I want to do, to teach me a lesson. I can see that the issue of racism in cricket has been covered less and less as time has gone on, because those whom the system benefits don't want the game to become a place for everyone. Some think the realities have been exaggerated and don't really accept or believe what people like me are telling them. There have also been active attempts to persuade journalists not to cover the story or reference things that have happened in the past or use words such as 'racism' when it comes to Yorkshire. This is what I must continue to battle.

I have a huge responsibility that's been given to me by Allah and it is one I will do whatever possible to fulfil. How I do this is a constant question I ask myself. I have the lived experience and I have the ear of people who can actually change things and, as a result, I'm in a unique position to platform the challenges and difficulties many people of colour face every day.

I understand how my story could be the catalyst for change, which is why I want to share it. It's the reason I am writing this book, and why I have started speaking at events. I want to make people aware of discrimination and how it can lead to racism, to understand what it's like to live in our shoes and from there have the uncomfortable conversations and important discussions about how we are collectively going to solve it. Far too often, solutions, as well intentioned as they are, don't really look at the wider picture and show no real courage to deal with tough structural problems. Instead, there is a focus on the superficial and the performative. It's not about what is perceived to be good, it is about doing good even if it's the hardest thing to do. That takes real courage.

We have to strive to find long-term solutions and we need to be unapologetic and impatient to make sure change happens. I'm proud of the fight that's happened over the last few years, and I wouldn't change anything that I've done. Allah knows that from day one all I've wanted to do is to make cricket better, and I hope we're on the journey to achieving that. The thought of my kids not being around cricket breaks me, but it also further drives me to look for solutions so that my children, Ayaan and Mirha, can enjoy the great game without the fear of being racially abused.

There have been many moments on my journey that have put life into perspective and taught me what really matters. A lot of people go their whole lives without finding a purpose and at the age of thirty-three, I'm lucky enough to have found mine. It's what drives me to get out of bed every day. My purpose is to ensure that nobody is subjected to being called a 'Paki' or any other derogatory name, and told it's just banter. It's time to create opportunities for everyone and level out the playing field. I want to ensure that everything I and others have gone through and the upheaval of my life was worth it. That can only happen if we have a game that is anti-racist. I'm a glass-half-full type of person, and so I truly believe we can get to a place where cricket is a space that is welcoming for all. To get there we must face the hard truths. I hope you will read this book willing to face up to them with me.

CHAPTER 1

Just a Kid from Pakistan

I was born in Karachi in Pakistan in 1991, the second child of five, with an elder sister and a younger brother and two younger sisters. I was a cheeky kid, confident and playful and full of energy. Except in the mornings. Mum would have to drag me out of bed, and I'd have to run to make the school bus on time. When I got home, I'd wait for the powerful sun to die down a bit, and then it was cricket until the end of the day. From an early age, cricket was everything to me.

Life was very family-oriented in Pakistan. As well as my mum, dad and siblings, my paternal grandparents lived with us too. There were more than a hundred flats in our block, which was in a prosperous part of the city, and there was a strong sense of community. I now look back at my early childhood with a lot of fondness. Life was good.

Big families were the norm: Mum had five sisters and a brother, and Dad is one of eight, with three brothers and four sisters. My dad's family was originally from India but moved to Pakistan after partition in 1947. Mum came from a fairly modest background. Her family were from a small village in Sindh province, where they were small-scale rice wholesalers. She knew how hard this was and how small the rewards were, and she was determined that her children were going to benefit from a good education. She was always pushing me to do my homework and read the Quran, and I have her to thank for the fact that I ended up with ten good grades in my GCSEs. Religion was just an accepted part of life. I prayed five times a day. I studied the Quran, often with my mum's sister, who was a schoolteacher, and we celebrated all the festivals together.

Dad started off working in a cassette shop before he moved to Bahrain to work in a bank. And then he married my mum – it was an arranged marriage – and moved back to Pakistan. He soon got into property and from then on worked really hard, becoming a partner in a successful construction and property firm. Mum was a housewife and the disciplinarian in the family, keeping us kids in check. Hard work and sacrifice were instilled in us but so was prioritising family; we would always do something together as a family on a Sunday, whether that was going to a kids' activity centre or a trip to the beach. Every couple of weeks we'd go to Pizza Hut, and we were always looking for new restaurants and styles of food to try. In Karachi, the street food is amazing, and it's constantly changing, so there was no shortage of options. And once a month, generally on a Friday, all of our extended family would get together. Our cousins were like brothers and sisters, too, and I fondly remember long evenings in restaurants and the whole family going out for breakfast together – happy memories.

People say that Karachi is a city that never sleeps, but that's not quite true. The only time people sleep is in the morning. I'd wake up for school, and it'd be so calm and quiet I could hear the birds singing. The rest of the time, it was a city full of hustle and bustle, always on the go, and people would stay up all night.

My waking hours were about playing cricket. We'd set up a game wherever we could find a spot to play, which was mainly on the streets in a little car park just outside the block of the flats where we lived.

By the time I was eight years old, I was playing alongside the older boys. I wasn't the best by any means – there were loads of talented kids – but I was massively competitive. Most days I would come home covered in cuts and bruises because I kept diving around on our concrete field.

A few cuts and bruises apart, it was a lovely place to live for a cricket-mad kid. The climate allowed us to play all year round, and there was always someone up for a game. I remember those baking days of mid-summer, when the temperature soars to over 40 degrees, and I was desperate for the sun to relent just a little so I could go outside. There were games available for people to play between each prayer: one after *Fajr*, one after *Dhuhr*, one after *Asr* and one after *Maghrib* and before *Isha*. A young kid in Pakistan plays much more cricket in a year than one of their contemporaries does in the UK, which I think allowed me to get ahead. In fact, when I was twelve, I had probably played more than an average fifteen-year-old would have in England. I was practising non-stop, and it meant I was developing my skills quickly and at a young age. More generally, I think this is why South Asian countries have greater success at youth cricket.

My dad was always very supportive of his children. When it came to me, family members would say to him, 'You're spoiling him. Stop letting him play so much cricket. You need to get him to concentrate on his studies.' Dad's response was always, 'No, let him play.' He believed in me, and I always managed to do really well in my exams, even better than my brothers and sisters.

It was actually my mum who loved cricket the most in our family, and she supported my dreams too (while also making sure I concentrated on my studies!). When I was out playing cricket, she'd be running around after me, trying to get me to go to my Quran tuition classes. I'd leave the flat with my school bag but find somewhere to hide it and go and play cricket instead.

It seems to me that my love for cricket was inevitable, as I was surrounded by it as I grew up. When I got home from school at about 3.30 p.m., and before it was time to go out and play, there was a highlights programme on, and my grandad and I used to watch it together. That programme and watching Pakistan play was what really got me into cricket at first. Then, every couple of months, there would be a tournament between different neighbourhoods or buildings, and my parents would always ensure a maid or driver would chaperone me so I could watch. You paid twenty rupees each and the pitch would be in a car park, roped off by bulb lights. Everyone would come to watch the game, and the atmosphere was electric. They used tennis balls wrapped up with white electrical tape. I would watch all night, desperate for the day I could play in one of these matches myself.

One of my early heroes was Imran Nazir, who played for Pakistan. It was his diving around the field that caught my eye, and it was probably the reason I did the same on our concrete pitches, although I'm sure he wasn't as covered in bruises as I was, not that I cared. I also used to throw a tennis ball at the wall in my bedroom and dive across the bed like he did. He was the coolest guy I'd seen, and I wanted to be like him. My other cricketing idol that I looked up to was Saqlain Mushtaq, the little tiptoe run-up, and big spin he would do was something I tried to copy as a youngster.

But the main role model in my life was my father. His resilience and hard work were instilled in all of us siblings, and I'm so glad they were, because I have needed them in abundance throughout my life: to help me when we first moved to the UK; to become a professional cricketer; to cope with the time when I was out of the game; and to weather the storm of the last few years.

Before my family and I moved to the UK in 2001, I visited a couple of times. I spent one summer living with my uncle in Hounslow in London for six months and went to Beavers Community Primary School, which was just across the road from his house. I'd race my elder cousin to and from the gate each day, and we spent our free time playing in the nearby park. I loved ten-pin bowling, and my cousin knew someone who worked at the local cinema, so we would get in free to watch all of the latest Bollywood films. It was such a great time.

I also used to go to Sunbury Cricket Club, where my cousins played. It was very different from playing cricket in the streets back in Karachi. I can remember two massive pitches, with kids running around all over the place when the junior sessions were taking place. It was the first time I'd used an orange windball, and we played a lot of Kwik cricket. The focus was very much on having fun. I wasn't the biggest of kids – I was stick thin and quite a lot shorter than some of those I played with and against – but I knew the game better than any of my contemporaries and felt I was ahead of most of them.

Cricket at its best has the ability to bring people together and build relationships for life. I have always been extroverted and I love being around people, so playing cricket was supposed to be me in my element in my safe place, even in a new country. And at that age, there was no sense of feeling that you didn't belong. Hounslow and London more generally are diverse places, but when you are a kid, you don't really see the colour of someone's skin anyway.

It was an amazing six months in which I got a taste of life in the UK. But I also very much missed my family, and when my visa ran out, I went home. The next time I visited, I didn't last more than a few weeks. I was too homesick. It's not that I didn't miss my family hugely during that first six months, it was just that I was younger and I was perhaps less aware of being away from home. When you're young, you're naive and sometimes there's no fear – you jump into everything, and if you get hurt, you pick yourself up and go again.

Pakistan was our home, and we were very happy there, but it wasn't long before our whole family was making the move to England, mainly as the result of two tragic events. On an evening that started just like any other, I came home from school, dropped my bag off, had a shower and some food, and made my way down to play cricket. But it wasn't like any other day. I was still inside the building, and my younger brother was outside playing, when I heard loud bangs in the street. Me being me, I decided to head towards the danger and have a look at what was going on. Loud noises, such as cars honking their horns and tyres blowing out, were pretty common, but these sounded different, and I wanted to know what they were, so I ran towards the sound and looked over a wall. People in the back of a car that was driving past were shooting at the kids out playing. I watched people being killed right in front of me. The scene was one of panic everywhere, and I ran home as fast as I could. My younger brother was picked up and brought inside by one of the elders from the flats. We were very lucky that we all survived, as we could all have been out there playing. It was a terrifying moment.

Unfortunately, this wasn't the only incident that made us begin to feel unsafe. The final straw for us was when one of my father's business partners was kidnapped and murdered by being set alight. When his body was found, there was only half of him left. We had often gone out for Sunday dinner with him and his family, and we were very close, so it was an incredibly shocking and upsetting moment. An image of my father sitting on a prayer mat and crying sticks in my mind even to this day.

At the turn of the century our home city was starting to become an unsafe place. It was the end of our life in Pakistan. Almost immediately, all three remaining partners decided to leave. The concern was the kidnappers would strike again. Apparently, their modus operandi was to target the oldest son of successful business owners – and I was my dad's oldest son – and there were rumours that they had inside assistance from the police. It was clear to us that the success my father and his business partners were enjoying was posing a risk to our lives.

The original plan was to go to Canada or the United States. But we went on pilgrimage to Saudi Arabia first and then visited family in England before deciding our next steps. It was a big decision to leave, but it felt like our safety had been compromised. I was ten years old and about to leave everything I had ever known.

CHAPTER 2
A Whole New Life

I clearly remember the day we left Karachi. We had decided to go to Mecca in Saudi Arabia first, then visit family in the UK before travelling on to Canada, so we all had our white *ihrams* on, the clothes that you wear when you're on your way to a pilgrimage. My grandparents were coming with us too, so all of our extended family and friends were there to see us off on the bus to the airport – it seemed like there were hundreds of people who had come to say goodbye. It was very emotional saying our farewells, not really knowing if or when we'd come back.

As a result of my parents' incredibly hard work, we had lived a very privileged life in Pakistan, and I understand now how difficult that must have been for my parents to leave behind. It showed me early on that sometimes you have to make tough decisions in life to build a better future.

Moving to a new country and leaving our friends and family behind was a daunting prospect, but as a ten-year-old, I also saw it as an adventure and was excited about what was to come. I think at that age I was old enough to understand what was going on but not old enough to be fully aware of the magnitude of it, and therefore less affected than, say, my elder sister was. As a result, I had mixed feelings. I was scared and anxious, but also excited. The way my parents protected us kids probably also played a part in making me feel secure about the move. However, looking back, I think leaving Pakistan did change my outlook on life, and I had to grow up a bit faster than I might have if we had stayed. I had a lot of freedom in Karachi, and was completely comfortable in my surroundings, so you could say that a little bit of my childhood was lost when we moved away.

Saudi Arabia was amazing. It's difficult to find the words to describe seeing Mecca for the first time. It gives me goosebumps just thinking about it now. I was full of energy and extremely thankful. Muslims believe that Allah calls you to his house, and not everyone gets the opportunity – some people are never able to visit – so I felt very privileged to be there. The pilgrimage is called the *Umrah*, and it consists of a number of rituals, including circling the Kaaba, the house of Allah at the centre of the mosque, seven times, and then at the end you have your head shaved, which is known as *Halq*. It was physically demanding, but you never felt tired – it really was an amazing feeling.

We stayed pretty close to Haram Sharif, the Great Mosque of Mecca. I'd wake up early with my dad and go for the *Fajr* prayer, then have breakfast and come back for a little sleep. The rest of the day was spent at Allah's house praying and feeling so thankful to be there.

My religion is extremely important to me. It shapes my life, informing my values and influencing my perspective on the things that happen to me. And it's what's kept me going over the last few years. Whenever life has been difficult, Allah has always said, 'Pray to me,' and I have left things in his hands. Believing that everything is planned and meant to be, and that Allah is looking out for me, is comforting. Praying the *namaz* (the five daily prayers), helping others, being compassionate, are all things that Islam preaches, and they can lead to inner peace and a feeling of connection, even when things are tough. And even though I might not have always been the perfect Muslim, my faith has brought me joy and solace, especially at times of celebration such as Ramadan and Eid. It has also provided me with the support of a loving community. These are the fundamental benefits of Islam, and some of the reasons why it is so important to me.

After Mecca, we paid a visit to Medina and al-Masjid an-Nabawi, the Prophet's Mosque, which was quite different to Mecca but just as impressive in its own way. We spent time praying and reflecting, and we felt very thankful to be there. We then headed off to the UK for a stopover to see my uncle and his family in Hounslow. It was July when we arrived, and London was covered in a sunny haze. I remember being picked up from Heathrow by my uncle and cousins. It was such a lovely moment for the whole family, especially Grandma and Grandad. We were always a close-knit family, so it was nice to be all together for the first time in a long time.

As we headed over to my uncle's house, I remember thinking that I really wanted some Fox's biscuits, which I remembered from my previous visits to the UK. Then, as soon as we arrived, it was out into the garden to play cricket. It was such a great few weeks, even if we were all a bit crammed into the house.

The plan was to emigrate to Canada, but during our time in the UK, my uncle suggested that we stay and seek asylum. It wasn't something my dad wanted to do, because you can't travel or work when you are an asylum seeker. He was a self-made person, having worked his entire life and always been the breadwinner. And, in the past, he had been the one to help his siblings and look after people who really needed it.

That sense of giving is something that has been instilled into us kids. The idea of not working and being at the mercy of others, therefore, really didn't sit well with him. But my uncle convinced him that England was the best place to be, and we ended up staying. For a start, we had family there, and that was so important to my mum and dad. Family was everything to them, which made it slightly easier to cope with the move. And although I was too young to be consulted, I was pleased we were staying in the UK, as I knew that I would be able to play cricket in my new country, which probably wouldn't have been the case in Canada. Cricket always came first for me.

The fact that there was a sizeable Pakistani community in the country also made the decision to stay that bit easier. People from the region had been moving to the UK since the days of the British Raj in the nineteenth century, but it wasn't until the partition of India and the birth of Pakistan in 1947 that migration really took off, with large numbers coming over in the 1950s and '60s in particular. Today, there are more than 1.5 million British Pakistanis, making the UK one of the largest communities in the Pakistani diaspora.

But despite this history, our introduction to life in the UK was not straightforward. When my father applied for asylum, on the grounds that his life and the lives of his family were in danger if we remained in Pakistan, we were moved to a hotel in London. It was massive, with hundreds of asylum seekers living there while their claims were being processed. We had two rooms, one small and one big, to accommodate all nine of us. With so many people from all over the world crammed into such small spaces, there was always a lot of noise in the hotel. People were constantly coming and going and there were many other kids just like me, with dreams and aspirations. Most of the residents were from war-torn countries. This experience of mine is why today I feel so disturbed hearing our politicians talk about refugees so negatively, as all it creates is hate and division. When you get to know people and don't label them as a faceless mass, you realise nothing is ever as simple as good and bad.

In the large reception area, A4 sheets of paper with lists of people's names would be posted every day, telling them where they were going to be housed on a more permanent basis. Because we had a big family, it was going to take longer for us to be rehoused than for some of the smaller families, so we just had to wait our turn. In the meantime, we'd go to the swimming baths, and we kids joined the local school. Even though we didn't know how long we were going to be there, we had to get on with life, and my parents tried to make things as normal for us as possible and shield us from any worries that they might have been experiencing. We were also grateful to be somewhere safe and away from the dangers that we had faced at home. And it was interesting to be surrounded by people from so many different places and cultures.

Being there did, however, make you appreciate everything we had in Pakistan and the sacrifices that our parents had made for us to be safe and have the opportunities to be successful in life. That's why everything that has played out since hurts even more. We went from having everything to having nothing. But Dad's always been a fighter, and he fought to build a new life for us. We leant on each other, and I think that period brought us even closer together as a family.

While we were still being housed at the asylum-seeker hotel, 9/11 happened. We all went to my uncle's house that day, and everyone was gathered in front of the TV. We couldn't believe what we were watching. It was one of those moments when life seems to stop right in front of you. It was a living nightmare being played out live on television.

27

Life changed for Muslims in the immediate aftermath – you could feel and see it on the streets. My father had a big beard at the time, and people started to call him Bin Laden when he was out and about, so we all tried to convince him to trim it. There was a lot of intimidation of Muslims, mostly out of fear and ignorance, and it was a scary time for us, especially when we were in a new country and in such an unsettled situation. It was tough, to say the least.

In retrospect, it also seems to me that this event was a turning point in how Muslims have been perceived and treated ever since, particularly in the Western world. Instances of Islamophobia have increased dramatically, and instead of society condemning this behaviour, we have leaders who greenlight and encourage it. It saddens me that we seem no closer to eradicating this type of hate and prejudice.

About a month after 9/11, in the October, after having been in the hotel for a few months, our names finally appeared on the piece of paper in the reception – we were going to Barnsley. We'd never heard of it and had no idea where it was, but on Halloween 2001, we took a bus from London. When we got to Sheffield, the bus emptied, and then we and another family, whom we spent a lot of time with, got taxis to Barnsley.

We moved into a house on Gawber Road, and that's where home has been ever since. It was a decent-sized house, particularly in comparison to the two rooms in the hotel. But it was a million miles away from our apartment in bustling Karachi. One of the first things we noticed was the silence – it was so quiet in this suburban neighbourhood, especially in the evenings, that we were all a bit unnerved.

Although we were pleased to be there, I won't say acclimatising to our new surroundings and a completely different culture wasn't challenging, because it was, especially for the first couple of years. We had gone from enjoying a privileged life in Pakistan to living in Barnsley, a town we knew nothing about, against the backdrop of 9/11. The weather was completely foreign to us, and winter nights were difficult, as was the fact that Dad wasn't allowed to work. In fact, it took seven years for his claim to be processed and all of us to be granted indefinite leave to remain, which must have been incredibly challenging for this man who had worked his whole life and always provided for his family. It was a shock to us kids too that we could no longer just get whatever we wanted – the first Eid was the first reminder of this for us kids as we would always get new clothes for Eid when we were in Pakistan, but circumstances meant we weren't able to afford new clothes that year. My parents did as much as they could, and moving country was another example of the huge sacrifices my dad in particular made for us, and something I've come to appreciate more as time has gone on, especially as I now have an insight into the mental toll that not being able to work can have.

But even though moving to a new country wasn't easy, this was our new home. It was the start of a new life, and we were determined to make the most of it.

CHAPTER 3

Early Cricket Years

The small-town anxieties of Barnsley were not something we were used to after the bright lights and vastness of Karachi and London. To illustrate the point: population of Karachi – approximately 18 million; population of Barnsley – approximately 250,000.

The first obstacle we faced was trying to find a mosque. It seemed to begin with that there wasn't one any more as the last one had been burned down in an arson attack, and then my father bumped into a local doctor at the bank who directed us to a local GP practice where another doctor had given up a room to serve as a makeshift place of worship. It was a far cry from Haram Sharif, but that is where we went for Friday prayers.

The next priority, at least from my perspective, was to find a cricket club. It didn't help that it was winter and the English cricket season was over, but we got out the *Yellow Pages* and found some options. The first one we went to was very small, so they suggested we try Barnsley Cricket Club instead. We drove over to the clubhouse but there was no one around, so we left our number and asked them to get back to us. It was weird not being able to play straightaway, and I spent the winter counting down the days until the weather improved and the new season began.

Third on the list of my priorities was school. I joined primary school in year six, my younger siblings were in the years below me and my sister was in secondary school. Luckily, I settled in quickly and made friends easily. My extroverted nature definitely helped when it came to moving to a new school in a new country. And being so into sport was also a good icebreaker.

Two of the main challenges we faced were acclimatising to the cold winter weather and dealing with our changed financial circumstances. But perhaps the most significant was moving to a small town where we didn't know anyone. Thankfully, our neighbours were brilliant, and they slowly but surely made us feel welcome and like we were part of the community. We lived in a really lovely area, and we'd give our neighbours gifts at Christmas and they'd do the same at Eid, and we'd make food for them – it was really nice. It also helped that there were a lot of kids in the neighbourhood, and our garden was one of the popular places to hang out. We'd play football and cricket in the back, and there were always lots of balls flying around everywhere, hitting windows.

Life began to fall into place, but there was one big thing still lacking: cricket. It had dominated my days in Karachi, so I was really missing it. Without cricket in Barnsley, life would have been a lot more difficult for me, and I'm not sure I would have been able to settle in as well as I eventually did. It was my first love, and it also gave me a little bit of an identity.

Luckily, my secondary school, when I moved there, was next door to Barnsley Cricket Club, and a lot of my friends at school played there. I was also very fortunate to have a teacher who loved the sport. In those days, at state schools, you were dependent on a teacher or parent to give up their free time to supervise extra-curricular activities, and Chris Rowbottom was that person at our school. He really encouraged me, setting up bowling machines for me to practise with. I also believe that his and my love for cricket contributed to loads of other kids at the school getting involved in the sport. He created incentives for getting kids engaged in the game by providing queue jumps for lunch for all those that wanted to play. Because of that, every day there would be seventy to a hundred kids, boys and girls from all years, playing cricket at lunchtime. It was great fun and a simple yet brilliant way to get more kids interested.

And that was what cricket was to me at that time: fun. I had played and watched a lot of cricket in Pakistan, but it was predominantly tape-ball cricket in the streets. It was only shortly before we'd left that I'd joined a club in Karachi and played with a hard ball for the first time.

When I joined Barnsley Cricket Club, I was doing well for them, and one of the coaches asked me if I'd like to go to some trials. I didn't know what the trials were for, but it was another opportunity to play cricket, so I said yes. That was the big difference between Pakistan and the UK. Whereas I played cricket every day in Karachi, there just weren't the facilities, the weather or enough people who wanted to do the same in Barnsley. It meant I never turned down a chance to play.

I got through the first and second rounds of trials and was then invited to attend some more at the cricket centre across from Yorkshire County Cricket Club at Headingley. It was here that the seeds were sown for the cricketer I was to become. At Barnsley, the juniors trained before the seniors. I was batting and bowling a bit of seam at the time, so I'd practise those skills in the junior nets. But because I wanted to stay at the ground and play for longer, I'd then bowl a bit of off-spin in the senior nets. When I went to the trials at Yorkshire, I saw myself as a seam bowler, but the Barnsley first-team captain, who worked at the cricket centre, came up and said, 'I thought you bowled spin?' When I said no, he said, 'I think you should.'

Because of this, I started to bowl some of my off-spin, and one of the coaches, almost as a joke, asked if I could bowl leg-spin too. I didn't really feel any pressure, because I still didn't exactly know what the trials were for, so I bowled a bit of leg-spin too and ended up doing a bit of everything that day. It went amazingly well, and I got through to the final trial, which was the first time my parents ever came to watch me play a proper game of cricket, rather than in the streets or the back garden. It was a lovely moment to have them there supporting me. Up to that point, I had travelled with one of my friends, but, unfortunately, he didn't make it beyond the semis.

Arriving for the final trials I had to ask the coaches what I should bowl and they told me to go with off-spin. I had a great day playing cricket and having my family with me. I left with a smile on my face and didn't give the chance of selection much more thought. Not long afterwards, a letter arrived to say that I'd been picked for the Yorkshire Under-12s. It was a big moment, but I didn't realise quite how significant it was until recently. My parents were struggling a bit at the time, particularly my father. Although we had a nice home and good neighbours, he was finding it difficult to settle into his very different life, especially because he still wasn't able to work. He was also facing overt racism after 9/11 which was incredibly damaging. There was one time he was called 'Bin Laden' in the street and because of this he started shaving his beard shorter. More abuse followed.

It was another normal day and after dinner together we headed to bed. In the middle of the night we were woken with a loud 'crash!' and discovered that two bricks had been thrown through a front and side window. Some of the glass landed in Grandma's room. We contacted the police but they didn't arrive until a lot later. Given the temperature of the world at the time, it is highly likely such an attack was racially motivated.

As a result of this incident, my mum and dad had been discussing between themselves about returning to Pakistan and had come to the decision that they wanted to go back. Before they could tell us what they had decided, the letter from Yorkshire arrived. Because of my selection, my family made a huge sacrifice, and we ended up staying. I'm immensely grateful to them, not only for making the decision to put me first, but also for keeping it from me, to spare me the pressure of knowing that we were only staying in England because of me. They eventually told me when I spoke out about the racism I'd experienced, which only added to the hurt I felt at that time.

Remaining in the UK wasn't the only sacrifice they had to make. One of the hardest things about playing cricket is the cost. As soon as you are picked you receive a letter outlining team kit costs and training costs. This is all before buying your own bat and other equipment. You also need to travel to games up and down the country. But Mum and Dad never complained or compromised when it came to providing me with the support I needed. For example, Dad sold some of his assets in Pakistan to raise money to buy a car, and they'd both get up early in the morning to prepare food for our days driving to wherever the cricket games were being held. A lot of energy and sacrifice went into helping me become a professional cricketer.

I also got to travel around a lot with the Yorkshire Under-12s. One memorable trip was to Ampleforth College in North Yorkshire – what an amazing place. I can't say I remember too much about the journey there because I slept most of the way, but when we arrived, we were met by beautiful, scenic views. It was in the middle of the summer, and it was the first time I'd been away from home without my parents. The team spent three or four days there, playing matches every day, and my parents travelled back and forth to support me. I performed really well and made some good friends. I even received a Gray-Nicolls cricket bag as an award for being the best bowler of the tournament, which was really nice. But I didn't need any prizes or the kudos of playing for Yorkshire – I did it because it was a means to playing another day of cricket, the game I loved so much.

CHAPTER 4

One to Watch

After getting picked for Yorkshire Under-12s, I continued to perform well and make progress as a cricketer. I was now concentrating mainly on off-spin, which I was good at, but, looking back, I do wonder if it would have served me better to not specialise at such a young age. Nowadays, coaching has developed a lot, and the prevailing thought is that it is better to learn a wide range of skills while you're still young. Regardless, I performed well, and I made my way through the age groups at the club.

Things really started to take off, though, when I was selected as the captain of the North of England Under-15s at the Bunbury Festival in Sussex in 2006, an event that was first held in 1987. Back then, it was sponsored by David English, who had at one time managed the Bee Gees and Eric Clapton. The English Cricket Board (ECB) took over the running of the tournament in 2018 and incorporated it into their Player Pathway programme, but even when I was playing it was considered the premier competition in the country for the best Under-15 talent and the first time that the England selectors took note of the players coming through. To give you an idea of just how much talent was on show that year, at the awards ceremony at the end of the week, I was named captain of an

All England XI that included future senior England captains Joe Root, Ben Stokes and Jos Buttler.

From then on, I was earmarked as a player who could go the whole way and make it as a professional. I was living the dream and threw everything into my cricket, with the goal of playing for England and being one of the best in the world.

From about the age of fourteen, I was also chosen to play for Yorkshire Academy and became more involved with the professional side. It was in the academy side a couple of years later when I first came across John Blain, who was brought in as the captain and coach. Straight from the jump, he tried to impose a 'do as I say' style of leadership. As a young spinner, I had always been encouraged to set my own fields and learn from my own decisions, good and bad, so that's what I wanted to do. I found it a bit strange, therefore, when this new captain came in and wouldn't let me, even though I had captaincy experience. I believe he had a problem with me from then on.

Even more of a problem, though, was the fact that he constantly used the word 'Paki' – he later argued that he thought it was just an abbreviation and was the same as calling an Australian an 'Aussie' or a New Zealander a 'Kiwi' – and I felt there was a difference in the way he dealt with me and the other South Asians in the team compared with the way he dealt with the white players, but as a young player, I just got on with it.

He was clearly struggling towards the end of his time at Yorkshire, when he went from academy coach and captain to the second XI coach and captain, and seemed like he wanted to start playing seriously again. There were young players in the team whom he was supposed to be developing, but John would bowl fifteen overs from one end, which was quite funny. He was supposed to be leading by example but I saw several instances in matches that weren't exemplary.

During my time in the Under-15 and Academy sides, I was performing well on a weekly basis and winning awards. I was voted BBC Young Sports Personality of the Year in 2006, named the Male Junior Sports Personality of the Year at the British Asian Sports Awards in 2007, and I was Academy Player of the Year in 2008. This was amazing recognition and motivation to keep working hard. This led to me making my senior debut for the Yorkshire first XI in June 2008. The weeks leading up to making my debut were incredibly surreal. Darren Gough was my first captain and would pick me up from my house to travel to away games.

I made my debut in a T20 game against Nottinghamshire at Trent Bridge. It wasn't my best performance, but I held my own, and we won, sending Yorkshire into the T20 Cup quarter-finals, which were due to be played on Monday, 7 July. It should have been a special moment for me that I could look at fondly, but it was overshadowed by the first controversy of my cricketing career. It all started when on the Friday before the game was due to be played, we found out that I wasn't registered to play for the senior side.

At the start of every season, each player needs to be registered with the ECB, but that year the administrator at the club who normally took care of the process was on maternity leave, and her replacement forgot to register any of the academy players. Things were further complicated by the fact that I didn't yet have my British passport. If the registration process had been done properly, I would have been given special dispensation to play, because I had come through the academy and school systems.

Despite the administrative error, the team expected the game to go ahead, so on the Monday afternoon the squad travelled to the Riverside Ground to take on Durham. It was a big game, and the Sky cameras were there. I wasn't in the team that evening, having just filled in for one game, so I was at home when I got a phone call at about half-four, a couple of hours before the match was due to start, telling me that the game had been abandoned and Yorkshire were more than likely going to be thrown out of the competition, which is what eventually happened.*

The next few days and weeks were very tough. I had my first taste of press intrusion, with reporters waiting outside my house, and one bloke tried to get in through the back garden. Luckily a friend came to our house to help move them away. I was a seventeen-year-old kid at the time, so it was pretty disturbing. It didn't help matters that Yorkshire's response seemed to create a narrative that I was somehow to blame, which I felt was insinuating that I had tried to hide my nationality from them. Martyn Moxon told Sky Sports at the time, 'As I understand it he was on our list as [a player] but as an academy player rather than a full-time player. He needed to have signed a piece of paper that he agrees to the rules and regulations of the ECB. Unfortunately, he [didn't sign it] and that's where the problem arose. Since then it appears his status in the country [is also] under question.' When I first signed on as a player at the club, I had to show them my Pakistani passport, so I had given them all of the relevant information, and I believe the mistake of not registering me lay with Yorkshire. As a result, I missed out on playing in the regional Under-17 tournament and for the England Under-17s over the next few weeks. That was really tough to take as I had

---

* The team were disqualified, and the result of the game I had played in was made null and void, which meant Glamorgan qualified for the quarter-finals instead of Nottinghamshire thanks to a superior run rate.

worked so hard towards both and was really looking forward to showing what I could do. It was extremely upsetting and disappointing, and I couldn't help but feel as though I had been fed to the wolves by Yorkshire. Looking back, it was probably the first indication of how quickly I could be made to feel other by the powers that be.

I had to go down to Lord's to get the special dispensation to play that I would have got if the registration had happened. The weird thing was, I had already played for and captained England age-group sides, and yet here I was, having to get dispensation to play for my county. It was unfortunate to have missed out on playing for England Under-17s, but, as I have done throughout my life, I didn't let it drag me down. I picked myself back up and continued to work towards my dream of playing for England.

Every time you put on an England shirt, no matter at what age group, it is an amazing feeling. The first time I was selected was when I played for the England Under-15 side and captained them in a tournament against Barbados Under-16s and Scotland Under-17s at Loughborough over a two-week period. It was an amazing experience – a bunch of fifteen year olds all living together and playing cricket in the summer. It was the first time I had come up against international opposition, which was a chance to test myself against high-level competition and see where my game was at. We had a lot of success and won every game, which I was really proud of.

We were coached by Richard Halsall, who went on to become the fielding coach for the senior England side for a while. I absolutely loved playing for him. Richard was actually quite a serious bloke, and I think we all feared him a little bit, but we also respected him because he treated us fairly, and he was improving us as cricketers.

My first experience of captaining was with the Yorkshire Under-15s, and I absolutely loved it. I played my best cricket when I was captain, because it stopped me from thinking too much about my own skills as a batter and bowler, and instead allowed me to concentrate on the tactical side of the game, which was a strength. I enjoyed being able to influence the game all the time, and it helped me to develop as a person and as a leader. My leadership style was to empower other people to make their own decisions and backing them even if things went wrong. It was also important to me that we enjoyed the game and played positively, always on the front foot. I was all about the kind of fearless cricket that England have become famous for in recent years. It was just a much more fun way to play.

In 2010, I travelled to New Zealand as captain of the England team for the Under-19 World Cup. We had an incredible side that included Ben Stokes, Jos Buttler, Joe Root, James Vince, Danny Briggs, Nathan Buck and Michael Bates, and we all got on really well. We were coached by the excellent Mark Robinson, whom I really enjoyed playing under.

Despite arriving in New Zealand in good spirits, and with real hopes that we could make our mark on the tournament, our preparations had been overshadowed by one of the strangest experiences of my cricketing career. I had captained the side for a couple of years and done it well. We'd had some success and liked playing with each other, but for some unknown reason the team manager decided there would be a secret ballot to choose who would captain the team at the World Cup. And although I won the vote, I felt like it undermined my position and potentially threw off our preparation. It just shows that people in leadership and decision-making positions can make some very strange choices when they feel under pressure.

Someone who thrived on pressure was Ben Stokes, who showed what a special player he was from the minute we landed in New Zealand. We were based in Christchurch, which is renowned as being one of the windiest cities in the world – flying in on a small aircraft wasn't for the faint-hearted. It took us all a few days to get over the jetlag, and then we had a few warm-up games. I remember watching Stokes hit cricket balls for what seemed like miles into the wind. It was incredible for a nineteen-year-old. And then he took that form into the pivotal game against India in the group stages. That India side had a lot of good cricketers in it, and they were one of the favourites to win the whole thing, but we played really well and managed to beat them by thirty-one runs, with Ben making a century.

Beating India meant we finished top of our group and qualified for the quarter-finals, where we would face the West Indies. When we woke up on the morning of the match, it was raining, and the forecast said it would continue all day. If the game had been rained off, we would have gone through, because we'd finished top of our group, whereas the Windies had come second to Pakistan in Group D. So, we were all hanging around at the hotel, not expecting to play, when the rain suddenly stopped in the afternoon and the game was on. It was still a bit overcast and wet as we made our way to the ground, but the conditions were good enough for us to play.

The West Indies had a couple of players who have gone on to be really successful, including Kraigg Brathwaite, the opening batsman, and Jason Holder, the all-rounder, both of whom have since captained the senior side. I dropped Brathwaite and he went on to score eighty-odd, which wasn't ideal. When we were chasing, we had a couple of unfortunate dismissals, and then Jason Holder bowled us out, getting five wickets. We were out of the tournament, which was really disappointing, because we had all the ingredients to go the whole way, but it wasn't to be. The silver lining is that a lot of the lads in that England team have gone on to win World Cups and Ashes series and achieve their cricketing dreams. I get goosebumps thinking about that – I'm incredibly proud of them, and of the fact that I got to captain them at that World Cup in New Zealand, which was such a fantastic experience.

The England Under-19s was a much more supportive and positive environment than the Yorkshire dressing room. We all got on and wanted each other to do well, perhaps because we were young and still had it all to do. At county level, you have a mix of ages, with people at very different stages of their careers. When you first come in, not a lot is expected of you, so people get behind you. But as soon as you start to perform, you are perceived as being a threat to the positions of the senior players. I think that's why the Yorkshire dressing room could be such a toxic place at times.

You see it a lot with older players who have been on central contracts for England, earning hundreds of thousands of pounds a year, and then they have to take a county salary, which is a huge drop. At the same time, their bodies and games are more often than not on the decline, so it becomes all about protecting themselves.

I might just have been a bit naive, but playing for the England Under-19s was the complete opposite of that. And although we didn't achieve what we wanted to in the World Cup in New Zealand, I felt secure about my place in cricket, and was confident that I would go on to bigger and better things with Yorkshire and England.

CHAPTER 5

The Year Everything Changed (2018)

Trigger Warning: Pregnancy Loss

It was 20 May 2018, and we had a One-Day Cup game against Warwickshire at Headingley on a beautiful, sunny day, with a big crowd expected. Since that disappointment at the Under-19 World Cup, I had enjoyed a good if slightly up-and-down career. I had also matured a lot, and was now married to the wonderful Faryal, who was expecting our first child in a couple of weeks.

I was always one of the first to get to the ground, and that day was no different. I hated being late, and I liked to have plenty of time to do my prep – a bit of bowling, some batting and all of my fielding drills – so that I would be ready to perform if selected. But Yorkshire had a lot of good players at that time, and, despite being fully prepared, I wasn't picked that day. After fulfilling all of my matchday duties, all that was left was for me to watch the game and offer my support to my teammates.

At Headingley, there is an inner and outer balcony where the players can sit. I was watching from the inner area when I saw Martyn Moxon, the Director of Professional Cricket at Yorkshire since 2007, answer his phone and stand up. And my stomach went. I don't know why, but I just knew something serious had happened. He pulled me to one side, along with Mark Arthur, the club's chief exec, and said that my wife had been taken to the hospital because there had been some complications to do with her pregnancy. And I just started to cry, because I knew that we had lost our unborn son.

Although I was in a daze, I managed to pick up my keys and run to my car. I remember screaming and hitting the steering wheel and crying very loudly on the forty-five-minute journey from Headingley to Barnsley Hospital. It felt like my whole world had been turned upside down. I was praying for a phone call to say that they'd found a heartbeat, but none came. And all the while I just kept crying and screaming and asking why this had happened to us.

When I got to the hospital, our whole family was there. As soon as my wife saw me, she ran to me, helplessly asking me to do something and then running to my dad and asking him to do something, saying, 'It can't be right. It's not possible.'

I had to stay strong for her and for the rest of my family, holding in my emotions as best I could. But after a while, I went outside and screamed really hard. I didn't know what else to do.

When I went back inside, my family tried to help us process what had happened and what needed to happen next. The baby had to come out, so we had to choose between a C-section and labour being induced. Neither was a good option, and it was the last thing I wanted my wife to go through when she was grieving and in shock, but we decided to go with the induction. We were told it would take two or maybe three doses of the drug to bring on the labour. But the maximum of three turned into twelve, and the next five days were a living nightmare.

I slept on the floor in the hospital room, and Faryal was hooked up to drips so she could receive the induction medicine, but it wasn't working, and her health began to deteriorate. Her temperature was falling and rising sharply, and the whole ordeal was taking a huge amount out of her. It was a really scary time, especially not knowing what was happening. The nurses tried to prepare us for what was to come, explaining that babies in this situation can be born covered in bruises or having lost a lot of their colour. And the longer the process went on, the higher the chance that something unusual might happen. But for the most part, we felt in the dark about what was going on.

About three days in, Faryal's temperature began to rise quite a lot, and this time it didn't come down. I began to feel real panic and was running around, looking for a doctor to help us, but the receptionist told me that none were available – it was beyond frustrating. I'd just lost my son, and I thought I was going to lose my wife as well. I was terrified.

I decided to ring Dan Jarvis, our local MP, to ask for help, and within five minutes, four senior people came in and made sure my wife's temperature came down. I actually feel quite lucky that I was able to think clearly enough to ring and that these doctors were available. I know people in hospitals see this sort of thing all day every day, but I'd just lost my son, and I needed support. It was really traumatic and disturbing.

After five days, we finally got the baby out. It was such a surreal moment. At first, I didn't want to see him, but Faryal wanted him on her chest. We named him Alyaan, and he came out looking like an angel – *farishta* in Urdu. He looked as though he was just sleeping. I remember my dad saying, 'I thought it was a boy.' It was almost as though he had lipstick on, and because of how beautiful and perfect he was, my dad thought for a moment that the baby was a girl.

Despite the heartache and how difficult this moment was, we were glad that the labour was over, and my wife was out of any immediate danger. It meant we could start to move forward. We spent some time in the hospital's Rainbow Room, a space for bereaved parents, and we looked at photos of our beautiful baby boy. The next day, I was able to take Faryal home before returning to the hospital with a baby basket so that I could bring our son home. What should have been a joyous moment was instead one of heartache.

I brought him to see my grandma and then took him to the graveyard. Lowering him into the ground was the most difficult thing I've ever done in my life. It's impossible to put into words the emotions that I was going through.

Only one teammate came to support me – I'll be eternally grateful to him for coming – but there were a lot of other people there, including my dad's friends and people from the mosque. The imam read a few prayers and I put our son into the ground and then went home.

The next few days and weeks and months were incredibly difficult. Not only was I grieving, but it was a massive wake-up call about the way I was being treated by Yorkshire. I'd been playing professional cricket for the county since 2008, with a small gap in between 2014 and 2016, and I'd been a part of the club for many years before that. But despite this, I came to the realisation that other people who had gone through tragedies had been supported. I, on the other hand, got very little help, and the only difference between them and me that I could detect was that they were white and I was not.

There was a real shift in my perspective and a recognition that I'd been looking the other way for so long. Microaggressions, overt racism, lack of opportunities, being held to a higher standard, every little mistake being picked out – I now feel the only explanation for them must be because I was a person of colour, a Muslim, a British Pakistani. It really changed the way I looked at the world. It made me realise that no matter what I did – and at various times over the years I'd sacrificed my own values and what I stood for in order to be accepted – it wasn't going to be good enough, and I was never going to be one of the team. I was always the outsider, the other, and that was simply because of the colour of my skin.

When you have spent the best part of a decade with team-mates, coaches and other people at the club, some of whom have stayed at my house and eaten my mum's cooking, and then they don't rally round and offer support, it really gets to you.

From the outside, I was living the absolute dream, playing professional cricket, appearing on TV and travelling the world. But I'd actually been struggling with my mental health for a long time, to the point that I had been taking antidepressants. And I finally realised why. I at last saw the system and Yorkshire County Cricket Club for what they were: racist. I could no longer ignore what was right in front of me – it was something that I was going to have to reckon with.

CHAPTER 6
Ten Years Earlier (2008)

A lot had changed in the ten years since I'd signed my first three-year senior contract with Yorkshire in October 2008. What an amazing feeling that was, realising I was going to be a full-time professional and be paid for doing something I loved. One of the most significant moments was getting a shirt with my name and number on the back. When you're in the academy and the second XI, your shirt doesn't have your name and number on it. It's a small thing, but it makes you feel like you're a part of everything, as do things like being included in the senior squad photos.

I really felt at that moment that I was on the way to achieving my hopes and dreams. And I was ready to sacrifice anything in my pursuit of being the best in the world and playing for England. And you do need to sacrifice a lot to become a professional cricketer. I'd go out running and work on my fitness instead of attending family events such as weddings and birthday parties.

Although I did well at school, it wasn't something that I was focused on, and I didn't spend a lot of time studying. I therefore initially decided that I wasn't going to go to college alongside playing for Yorkshire. However, after a few weeks, I had a change of heart, partly because I realised that in the winter, especially back in those days, there was not a lot to do when you were a professional cricketer, and I thought it was important that I use my time wisely. But the dream was still to be the best cricketer I could be, and I was prepared to do anything to achieve that dream, even though there were challenges that came with that.

Looking back, I'm not sure that my approach was the right one, especially from a mental health point of view. Sacrifice and hard work are important, but there also has to be a good life balance. I was just a teenager, after all. I guess that's something a lot of professional sports people struggle with, because it's so cut-throat, and you are always looking for that 1 per cent advantage.

Me signing a professional contract was massive for my family as well. Even though I didn't find out until much later about my parents staying in the UK to allow me to pursue my cricketing dreams, I was fully aware at the time of my responsibilities as the eldest son. My father's health wasn't great, and the period of not working had had a big effect on him. I thought it was my responsibility to look after him, and the rest of my family – my mum and grandparents and siblings – and I tried to do that to the best of my ability. Initially I stayed really strong on my values but subconsciously I felt that I wouldn't progress until I started fitting in. To achieve my dream, I was pulled away from the family values that had been nurtured in me which is something I deeply regret.

Looking back, the stars in the Yorkshire dressing room, many of whom were my heroes, blinded me to the overt racism that I was being subjected to from the very outset of my career. Things like being called a 'Paki' or a group of Asian lads being told to go and sit over there, there being near the toilets. These were the sorts of things that Matthew Hoggard later admitted were commonplace in the Yorkshire dressing room.

Another racist term that was used frequently was the word 'Kevin', which was used in reference to all people of colour and I spoke about this at the DCMS select committee in 2021. When I first raised this at the SPB investigation and the employment tribunal, Yorkshire initially denied that anyone had ever used the term. But further down the road, that response was corrected, and they admitted that it had been used. Professional Cricketers' Association vice-chair and Derbyshire player Anuj Dal also told the DCMS committee that 'Kevin' was used as a derogatory term for non-white players, and that it had been used outside of Yorkshire. There were never any investigations done into the use of the word 'Kevin' throughout the county game.

In contrast to this, I was also contacted after DCMS by Warwickshire County Cricket Club CEO Stuart Cain because Tim Bresnan was now a Warwickshire player, and we had a very good conversation. I said to him, 'Ultimately, you've got to do what you've got to do, but from my point of view, I'd love to sit down and talk it over with him, and if there's an apology, it will be fully accepted by me.' If there was any organisation that handled this stuff with respect, it was Warwickshire under Cain. He was professional, authentic and straight, and he backed up his words with actions – to me, that's what genuine leadership looked like.

Back then, derogatory comments like 'Paki' and 'Kevin', and being made to feel other, clearly had an effect on me. Most of the time it was without me even realising. I was so determined and focused on being the best that I looked the other way. Despite the abuse, thanks to my own hard work and dedication, I slowly but surely became a part of the squad and then the team. I made my List-A and first-class debuts in 2009, and I scored a century in my second first-class game, against Worcestershire in June of that year. At just eighteen years and 112 days old, it made me one of the youngest players ever to score a century for Yorkshire. We were really up against it when I went in at number nine, and Worcestershire started bowling short balls at me, hitting me on the head. But I weathered the storm and began to play my shots. It was such a good feeling when I hit a four to take me to a hundred off just ninety-two balls.

I also played for England Under-19s against Bangladesh during the summer, and I performed really well, taking six wickets at Scarborough and then five at Derby in the two Test matches we played. I was England Under-19 captain for the One-Day Internationals that summer and for our tour to Bangladesh before we played in the 2010 Under-19 World Cup.

But it wasn't all plain sailing. Later in 2010, in a series against Sri Lanka Under-19s, I was dropped by team manager John Abrahams after breaking a curfew, as was my teammate Atif Sheikh. Although I got on well with John, and had even made a video in support of his wife Debbie, who is a Labour MP, I was really stupid and made some regrettable comments about him on Twitter, which I immediately deleted after I realised they were viewable by the public. Social media was in its infancy, and I didn't properly understand how Twitter worked – I only had about three followers – but that's no excuse, and I was rightly held accountable for my actions, with Yorkshire suspending me and the ECB giving me a one-month ban.

With that said, I do feel that a bit of a double standard was applied. That night at the hotel, I was actually trying to calm things down, but the next day Atif and I were singled out. And if you compare that to an incident on our tour to Bangladesh with one of the players, what we did was much less severe.

But John, who is a person of colour, fought tooth and nail to keep that lad there. If you put the two situations side by side, the only obvious difference is one incident involved someone who was white and the other two people of colour. I was playing in the Yorkshire second XI at Loughborough University a few years later, and he apologised to me for the way he had handled things.

Some believe that race cannot be a factor when it comes to people of colour's decision-making. To be clear, I'm not saying that was what motivated John when he dropped me and Atif, but I do think it's important to challenge the myth that a person of colour can't act in a prejudiced or biased way. I see this excuse used all too often by institutions and organisations, and we're seeing it play out in our political spectrum right now. If a person of colour is in a position of power and making the decisions, it shouldn't mean that they can treat other people of colour, or other people from minority backgrounds, however they want and not be held accountable for it.

After that controversy, what came next couldn't have been better timed. I had my first experience of playing grade cricket in Australia. I spent the winter in Perth and had probably the best three months of my life. I was playing cricket, making new friends and growing up. But what was a fantastic experience was overshadowed by a family loss.

My grandad had been ill for a while before I left, so when I said goodbye to him, I had the terrible feeling that it might be the last time I saw him. I was still incredibly close to him – we continued to share our deep love of cricket – so it was a heart-wrenching moment. I've got good memories of the last time I saw him, but while I was out in Australia, he passed away. My family didn't want me to come back early, so they decided they weren't going to tell me until I came home a couple of months later, but I knew there was some-thing wrong. I don't know how, but during the time that my grandad passed away, I was struggling to sleep and felt that something definitely wasn't right. Over the course of the next week, I kept ringing home and asking if everything was OK, but they didn't say anything. I wasn't convinced, though, so I booked my flight and came back.

My uncle came with my dad to the airport to pick me up, which was unusual, so I knew my feeling that something was up had been correct. When I arrived home, my suspicions were sadly confirmed when I saw a lot of Qurans on the table.

After the death of a Muslim, people come and visit, and we read the Quran together as part of the mourning process. But despite the support of my family and community, I took his loss hard and struggled for quite a while. As you get older, you realise that these things are a part of life, albeit perhaps the most difficult part, and you have to take consolation that your loved ones have gone to a better place and move forward. And that's what I tried to do, but I did struggle with my grief to begin with.

Thankfully, I soon had more cricket to take my mind off things. At the beginning of the 2011 season, I was sent on loan to Derbyshire, which was probably the most fun I've ever had playing cricket. The loan came about after Derbyshire expressed interest in me and then scouted me at a second XI match, something that John Blain wasn't happy about, even though it was all above board and sanctioned by management. The month I spent there was incredible. John Morris, Derbyshire's head of cricket, and team captain Luke Sutton made me feel really welcome. Luke basically said to me, 'Just do whatever you want to do. If you do it with a smile on your face, we're going to back you.' I played three County Championship games and five forty-over matches. I was having success and enjoying playing there, but the loan ended and I was back at Yorkshire. I felt appreciated and wanted at Derbyshire, so it was difficult leaving so soon.

Fortunately, when I came back to Yorkshire, I had some amazing performances. One in particular stands out: a T20 game against Lancashire. Yorkshire had always struggled with the T20 format, as the club was quite traditional and could be a bit boring and backward at times. But I loved T20 and was good at it, so they put me straight into the side for the game at Old Trafford. I did really well with the ball, taking three wickets for just fifteen runs across my four overs, and then I scored eleven not out with the bat to win us the game and earn myself the player-of-the-match award in front of a packed house. In the week leading up to the match, we practised scoop shots for the first time, and during my innings, I scooped one ball and reverse-scooped another. It was an incredible feeling.

I ended that year by signing a two-year contract extension. In retrospect, I wish Derbyshire had done more to make it clear that they wanted to sign me, and I could have played out the rest of my career there instead, but everything happens for a reason, and playing for Yorkshire is an incredible honour. They are one of the biggest clubs in the country, and when you have success at Yorkshire, you have a great chance of going on and playing for England as well.

Despite playing well and earning a new contract, the 2011 season was not a good one for the club as a whole. There was quite a bit of in-fighting amongst the coaching staff, which included John Blain, Steve Oldham, Kevin Sharp, Craig White, Ian Dews and Martyn Moxon. It wasn't the best environment to be in, if I am being honest.

There were issues amongst the players too. The 2010 season had been a really successful one for a lot of individuals. They'd done well for Yorkshire and a lot of them had subsequently been picked for the England Lions. They were all in that head space of wanting to play for England, and it seemed as though their priority wasn't Yorkshire. It felt to me like a more selfish and individual-oriented environment.

As a result, there was a massive clear-out of the coaching staff before the 2012 season, with only Martyn Moxon and Ian Dews remaining at the club. Jason Gillespie was appointed first-team coach and Paul Farbrace coach of the second XI, and they were both like a breath of fresh air. Jason was coaching in Zimbabwe that winter when he was given the job, but he came over to see us and said, 'We're going to work really hard, but we're also going to have a lot of fun.' And Paul's first indoor training session that winter also sticks in my mind. Martyn Moxon said we could book our batting sessions with Paul or with him, and the whole room went to Paul. It was quite an awkward moment, because it was obvious how uncomfortable Martyn was, but it was also pretty telling of how fed up people had got with him and his way of operating and showed how much the players were looking for new and better inspiration.

I got on with Paul straightaway and really enjoyed playing for him. I think he's one of the best coaches I've ever worked with. He gave me the freedom to go out and play my own game. As the 2012 season began, I was in the second XI, but Paul really backed me to push on and make a case for promotion to the first XI. I was scoring runs batting at number three and taking wickets, and my form meant I was soon selected in the first team for a County Championship game against Northamptonshire, and I just went from strength to strength from that point onwards. It all came from the belief Farbie had in me. He also played a big part in our change in mindset when it came to T20 cricket in 2012, which led us to making it to finals day for the first time. I really valued my relationship with him.

Sadly, since my speaking out, we've not had much contact. A lot of people would rather look the other way and try to pretend racism is not happening, perhaps because one of their friends is implicated. I hope that's not the case with Paul, but we've had little or no communication, which is disappointing, because he was such a big advocate for me as a cricketer, and the backing I had from him was incredibly helpful.

He lived near Barnsley, so we used to travel together quite a lot to training and games. I remember him telling me during the 2013 season, when we were in the car one day, about the issues that he was having because the other coaches suddenly felt threatened by his presence, and they were using him less and less. It was no surprise to me that he ended up leaving and winning the 2014 T20 World Cup with Sri Lanka and then going on and being part of a very successful England set-up. Trevor Bayliss and Eoin Morgan receive a lot of praise for the way they turned England around at limited-overs cricket, and rightly so, but even before Trevor came in, there were one-day games when England scored 400 runs, and while I wasn't in that dressing room, I have absolutely no doubt Farbie would have played a big part in that.

Everyone has their strengths and weaknesses. After leaving the England set-up, he joined Warwickshire as their sporting director, and he seemed to find that role more of a challenge. I think that was because first and foremost he's a coach. He's a person who likes to get on the ground and work with the players directly, so I'm pleased to see him back doing what he's best at, now he's the head coach at Sussex. It's certainly been interesting to follow his journey from afar. From a personal and cricketing point of view, I thought he was absolutely outstanding.

Jason Gillespie was also someone whom I got on with and respected. In 2013, after the pre-season tour, I had a conversation with him in one of the rooms in the new Headingley stand, and I wish I'd opened up to him more then. He talked to me about how it can be difficult when you have injuries and that it's not easy to manage the expectations of the coaching staff. I don't know what came over me, but I burst into tears, and he gave me a hug – that's something I'll always be thankful for. I can't help but think, knowing what I know now, that if I'd told him then what I was going through, things would have got better.

In 2018, there was some talk about me potentially going over to join him at Sussex, then, in 2020, after I spoke out, he rang me, and we had a really good conversation. He talked about how disappointed he was that he was the coach during some of the periods when I was having such a hard time, and I appreciated that.

I did Cricket Australia's *Cricket Connecting Country* podcast with Jason in October 2020, and he did an interview with ESPNcricinfo after I spoke out. In the podcast, he spoke about his reaction to my media interviews revealing what had happened to me during my time at Yorkshire. He shared how it was heartbreaking and quite upsetting to learn I was subjected to institutional racism during his tenure as coach. He said he had noticed I was struggling but wasn't aware it was because of the racism I had experienced. It was a confronting and eye-opening moment for him.

By the middle of the summer, the T20 competition had begun. As I said before, Yorkshire had never had much success in the format, despite having good players and strong teams over the years. As a result, Jason and Paul brought new ideas and tactics with them, and they really tried to change the mindset of the players when it came to playing T20 cricket. However, some of the players didn't want to take on board what they were saying, including, it seemed to me, Ajmal Shahzad. Ultimately, Jason and Paul wanted the team to play in a certain manner, but I wondered if some individuals resisted that because they'd enjoyed individual success. The question that was asked of them was, 'Well, how successful has the team been?' Most players could see their point and bought into the new ideas, but my sense was that Ajmal didn't, and that could be why he was quickly moved on. It was widely reported that Colin Graves had said about Ajmal, 'I am not prepared to have somebody playing for Yorkshire who does not want to be part of the team.'

The first game of the 2012 T20 Cup was against Durham at Headingley. We were chasing a score of 142, and we were twenty-three for three when Joe Root came in and hit three fours in quick succession. That was the mindset we wanted to play with at the time. The other one-day and white-ball teams in the country were a lot more attacking, and we wanted to play a similar brand of cricket, never taking a backward step and backing ourselves that nine times out of ten it would work out for us. When batting, we'd look to hit every ball for six, and if not six, then four, then three and so on. That day, Rooty put the plan into action, and we got really close, losing by just two runs. I had gone in towards the end of the match, and I'd been brave, playing my shots. It had looked like we were well on our way to winning the game, but Ben Stokes stopped a four that I thought touched the rope, and there was a controversial decision about a wide, which meant we came up short. The positive thing was that we had changed our mindset, moving away from the usual nudging and nurdling that would normally see us get nowhere near the total we were chasing, and instead putting us in a position to potentially win the game.

At training after that loss, Andrew Gale suffered an injury, and Jason Gillespie asked me to captain the side, which was an incredible honour. I was really looking forward to my first game leading the team up in Durham. We set a good score of 171, and we had a plan of how we were going to go about our business in the field, but Durham looked like they might chase it down. I made a couple of moves, and we ended up winning. After that, we didn't lose another T20 game through the group stages. We finished runners-up, which was a pretty incredible turnaround in the club's T20 performance. We had never reached finals day before.

I'd broken into the first team and was doing really well in the County Championship, and I was the youngest ever captain of a senior Yorkshire side, one that included Adil Rashid, Mitchell Starc, Joe Root, Jonny Bairstow and Ryan Sidebottom, and the first of Asian heritage. Then at the end of the season, we had a game against Essex at Chelmsford that would see us promoted to the First Division if we won. I played a prominent part, scoring a fifty in both innings, including seventy-five not out during my second outing at the crease, and I took three wickets in the first innings and a five-for in the second to help us win the match. I was then picked for the England Performance Programme tour to India and I was also invited to the senior England team's training camp in Dubai just before they went to India for a Test series.

I really was living the dream. Or at least that's what you would think. After the game finished in Chelmsford, we all headed out to a local nightclub called Sugar Hut. On the way back that evening, I cried my eyes out in a taxi with Steve Patterson. I don't think he knew how to react – he probably just put it down to us having had a drink. To be honest, I probably did the same, as I thought that putting a brave face on how I was feeling and moving on was the way to go. Later, when I spoke out, he sent me a supportive message and apologised to me on a call.

It should have been the happiest day of my life, because everything that I'd been working towards was starting to come to fruition. But something was bugging me. And what that something was only fully came to me in 2018.

CHAPTER 7
Assimilation and Othering (2012–14/15)

Trigger Warning: Suicidal Thoughts

When I first started to play professionally for Yorkshire, I was very confident and assured, perhaps even borderline arrogant. Part of this stemmed from a feeling that I belonged in the team from a cricketing perspective, but I also took pride in and strength from my religious beliefs and culture.

If the team went on a night out, I wouldn't drink. Even when I was in Perth in Australia playing club cricket, I was always the designated driver. I didn't feel the need to drink, so I didn't. But before long, I began to feel, perhaps subconsciously, that I needed to fit in more to ensure I got the same opportunities as my contemporaries to play and progress.

But even though I started to go out and drink with my teammates, I was still made to feel like an outsider. If I was talking to a girl in a nightclub, my teammates would come up and say, 'Why are you talking to him? He's a Paki,' something Gary Ballance later admitted to. And it wasn't just my teammates who would direct racial slurs at me when we were out drinking – other people at the cricket club would too. I was just trying to fit in and be one of the lads, but it didn't seem to make a difference, and my confidence took a hit.

Looking back, the pressure to fit in while still being othered had a big effect on me, and I now understand that the emotions I felt in the taxi at the end of the 2012 season were a reaction to this. It all came out, but, as I said, I didn't really know why I was crying at the time.

After the taxi incident, I travelled to South Africa to play for Yorkshire in the Champions League. We had to win a couple of qualifying games to get into the main tournament, which we did, against all expectations. We then got to play against some of the top teams from other domestic competitions around the world, including IPL sides the Mumbai Indians and the Chennai Super Kings, who had the likes of Rohit Sharma, Harbhajan Singh, Sachin Tendulkar, M. S. Dhoni and Suresh Raina playing for them, and the Sydney Sixers, who had Mitchell Starc, Shane Watson, Brad Haddin, Josh Hazlewood and Pat Cummins in their team. It was incredible to be competing against players of that stature.

One of our games was against the South African side Highveld Lions at the Wanderers Stadium in Johannesburg. Mumbai Indians were playing Chennai Super Kings straight after our match, so we had to leave the dressing room as quickly as possible, but I was feeling a little bit ill that day and was slow to get out of the shower. As I was coming out, everyone else had gone, and there in front of me was the great man himself, Sachin Tendulkar. I was standing there in a towel thinking, 'Oh my God, what am I supposed to do?'

I was completely star-struck, but I quickly got dressed and went over to speak to him and ask him for a shirt. He didn't have one to spare, so instead he gave me a signed pair of his blue gloves. It was a huge moment for me to meet one of the best ever to play the game and capped off what was an amazing experience overall. What we expected to be a two-week trip ended up being nearly five and a half weeks and became one of the biggest highlights of my career.

After the Champions League, I then moved on to Dubai for a three-day camp with the full England team, which was an amazing experience. I was rubbing shoulders with players in the great England Test team that went to India and won, including Jonathan Trott, Alastair Cook, Jimmy Anderson and Stuart Broad. It was incredible.

I was also picked to play for the England Performance Programme, and we had a tour of India that winter of 2012. This was when Ben Stokes and I got to be twelfth man at the Mumbai Test match. I remember joining the England team at the Taj. Making my way to the ground with the team was an incredible experience and something I treasure. I had enjoyed a breakthrough season, and I'd done well in the Champions League, but it had taken a toll on me, and I was physically and mentally tired. When you add in the impact of trying to fit in and all the abuse that was coming my way, I was not in the best shape, and I spoke to management to let them know that I was struggling and needed to rest. Unfortunately, I felt this was ignored.

On the first day of the first game, I dived to stop a ball and my knee got stuck in the ground. I had to have an X-ray, which showed some damage, so I left the tour with an injury, returning to Yorkshire to rehab and try to get fit.

In March 2013, we had a pre-season trip to Barbados. I didn't feel like my knee had fully recovered yet, and I'd turned my ankle shortly before we left, so I wasn't sure how much I was going to be able to participate in the matches. We were out one night in St Lawrence Gap, and someone said that I was unprofessional and needed to sort my lifestyle out. As you can probably imagine, I was extremely frustrated. It was a private conversation between the two of us, and we would have sorted it out if we had been left to our own devices. But then Andrew Gale came in from nowhere and started shouting at me. I told him to stay out of it and that it had nothing to do with him, but that altercation caused big issues between us from that point onwards.

Andrew could be quite a forceful and intimidating person, and because of this I always felt a bit scared to be around him. There was one incident with Adil in particular that stands out. When no action was taken, Adil did an interview saying that unless Yorkshire started to treat him right, he would be looking for another club, which caused a massive fuss.

To begin with, I put Andrew's behaviour down to him feeling threatened by me, particularly after I had taken over captaincy of the T20 side in 2012. After he was injured and I took over from him, we went undefeated until the final, when he came back in and captained. But it wasn't just the fact that we won when I was at the helm; it was the way we were winning. Suddenly, we were playing a completely different brand of cricket. As a result, I had people at the club coming up to me and saying off the record that they thought I should be made the permanent captain of the limited-overs sides. It was often that way at Yorkshire – there were a lot of whispers and rumours rather than people being direct and saying what they thought.

The day after Andrew had a go at me in public in Barbados, Martyn Moxon, Jason Gillespie and he had a chat with me, and I was blamed for causing the argument and accused of drinking too much and not looking after my body – basically, I was made to feel like it was all my own fault, something that I had to get used to over the years. I found the whole trip really difficult. When you think of Barbados, you think of sun, sea and sand, but I was feeling really down, and there were a couple of days when I didn't even get out of bed. I was battling with the guilt of having started drinking in order to fit in, even though it was against my values and my religion. I felt like I was letting people down, and it was having a negative effect on me. Then there was the contrast of having had an unbelievable season, in which I had captained the club in the T20s, and having the club captain screaming at me in a public place with lots of people there.

Sometimes people lose their cool in the heat of the moment, but this wasn't an isolated incident. I felt as though the micro-aggressions and everyday racism were occurring regularly, and although most examples weren't particularly significant on their own, they were all adding up to make me feel as though I was different. In retrospect, I can't think of another time when someone in a similar situation to me, trying to come back from an injury, was shouted at in a public place and then blamed for it the next day. It was really tough.

When we returned to England, my knee still wasn't right, so I went for another scan, and the decision was made that I needed to have surgery. As a result, I lost my place in the team and was feeling really down. The night before my surgery, I wasn't thinking straight, and I climbed over the railings of the balcony of my flat in Barnsley and thought about throwing myself off. Luckily, I hadn't been drinking, and I was able to think a little bit more clearly before doing something stupid. I thought of my cousin who had died by suicide, jumping off a four-storey building, and the effect that had had on his mum and dad. I also thought about my religion, and how suicide is forbidden. And I thought about how I didn't want to let my dad down. So, I climbed back, came inside, closed the doors and cried my eyes out. I was scared of what I was doing and what was happening to me. How had I gone from the highs of the 2012 season and being on the verge of the England first XI, when I was twelfth man for the Test match in Mumbai, to standing on the other side of the railings, contemplating ending it all? It was a really tough moment, but, yet again, I tried to put a brave face on it and didn't share with anyone what I was going through.

I can still feel what it was like that evening on the balcony, and the knowledge that the outcome could have been very different haunts me to this day. I feel incredibly lucky to be here, though sadly this wouldn't be the last time I would feel the world is better off without me in it.

CHAPTER 8
Taking a Break (2014)

Although I performed admirably in white-ball cricket during the 2013 and 2014 seasons, I had lost confidence in myself as a person, and I'd lost confidence in my body. I also thought the club captain hated me, and that I wasn't welcome in the dressing room. There was a constant battle going on inside me, and it had got so bad that during my morning journey from Barnsley to Headingley, I would daydream of being in a car crash so I could have a reason to have a few weeks off. I was struggling badly. But once I got back from injury, I continued to play to the best of my ability, as I always did, despite all of my off-field struggles.

Towards the back end of the 2013 season, Nottinghamshire approached me and offered me a three-year contract. Because of the way I was feeling, and how much I was struggling in the increasingly difficult environment in Yorkshire, I was keen to go. I thought a fresh start somewhere else might be just what I needed. But Yorkshire didn't let me explore it. Jason Gillespie emailed my agent that he wasn't happy that I'd spoken to another club, and then Martyn Moxon got me in and said, 'We back you.'

I wish I'd had the confidence to follow my gut, because I genuinely feel like it was exactly what I needed. And lo and behold, as soon as the 2014 season started, I could tell that Yorkshire were going to get rid of me. Sure enough, towards the middle of the season, Martyn Moxon called me to say I was being released. It was a devastating blow.

I trained a little bit with Derbyshire, and I was going to sign with them, but I knew deep down that I needed a break from the game instead. I needed to get off the treadmill, but it was still an extremely difficult decision to make. For as long as I could remember, I had been known as Azeem Rafiq the cricketer – it was a huge part of my identity. This happens to a lot of sports people when they stop playing – a big part of who they are is lost.

All athletes know that their playing days are going to finish at some point. Some have achieved everything they wanted to and enjoyed long, successful careers. These lucky ones are more likely to be financially stable and have clear goals about what comes next. But for others, the end comes prematurely, or out of the blue, and they are just not ready for what comes next. For those people, it is much harder to cope with the end of their playing careers.

When you're playing, you have all this attention on you. People want to know you and be around you. And then suddenly it's gone. Your phone doesn't ring any more, and when you call people, they don't pick up. Little things like that can really get to you. It's also easy to make some bad decisions and end up in financial difficulty. And having no clear sense of purpose is also a real problem. All your life, you've been told where to be, what to do, what to wear, and all of a sudden you've got to map out your day, your week, your month. This can be really difficult for a lot of people.

It was no different for me. I didn't expect to be out of cricket, and effectively out of a job, at such a young age. I moved back in with my parents and didn't leave my bed for days. I didn't have enough money to put petrol in my car, but I was too embarrassed to ask my dad for help. I ended up doing secret customer visits at leisure centres to earn a bit of cash.

But despite how difficult it was, I tapped into my resilience, and as time went by, the easier it became and the better I felt. I was getting back to my own values and being the person I wanted to be. Removing the constant abuse and racism, and not being called the 'Paki' and being othered, was ultimately beneficial to my state of mind, even if I didn't fully realise that that was the issue in the first place. In retrospect, it seems obvious that feeling like I could have been dead in the corner and no one would have cared, was clearly not a good place to be.

Things really started to improve when I got married in Pakistan to my lovely wife Faryal in the winter of 2015. It was an arranged marriage, which is something that I was keen to pursue, because I spent so much time concentrating on my cricket that I had no real social circle outside of the game through which I could meet people. We were introduced in 2014, and we then spent time getting to know each other, during which time we developed a close bond and knew that we wanted to get married. I think there is a misconception about arranged marriages in the West that the bride and groom have no choice in the matter and don't really know one another when they get married, but that is just not the case. It works more like friends or family playing Cupid and making introductions. It was very much up to us to then see if we wanted to take it further, and we were the ones who made it happen.

It was a massive Asian wedding, with multiple events and me arriving on a horse, which was quite an entrance. The *mehndi* is a big dance, with the two families competing against one another, and there was lots of amazing food on offer, although Faryal and I were kept so busy with photos and mingling that we didn't really get a chance to enjoy it, which was a shame.

Before and after the wedding, I spent some time coaching for a private academy out in Dubai. When I returned to the UAE after getting married, the England Lions were playing there, so I was able to reconnect with Peter Such, the National Lead Spin Bowling Coach, spending a day with him. It was an important step in the process of picking myself back up and getting myself playing again. Afterwards, Peter invited me to come and bowl at the team, which I did, and it went really well.

Faryal joined me for the second half of my three months in Dubai, and with her support, along with doing the coaching and bowling and generally trying to rebuild my cricket, I was able to restore some of my confidence. We'd applied for a British visa for her, but it hadn't come through yet, so after Dubai she returned to Pakistan, and I went to the UK, which wasn't ideal, but we were confident that it would be a temporary separation.

Visa difficulties and delays are things that Muslim people have become very accustomed to since 9/11, and whenever I travel with a white person, they are shocked by the extra checks and scrutiny that I come under as a person of colour in airports. It's why I find it frustrating when some white people push back at the label of privilege, citing their own individual experiences of hardship. Systemic racism is not about what one person goes through; it is indicative of discrimination at a societal level. And, yes, you might have worked hard to get where you are, but you have not had to overcome the kinds of racism and Islamophobia that are commonplace for people like me. Whenever I enter a shop, there is a good chance that the people working there are looking at me as a potential thief. Similarly, when I'm at an airport, I know that the security staff are probably viewing me as a potential terrorist. The starting point for a white person is completely different, and that is the definition of privilege in my eyes.

After the Dubai trip, when I was back in England, I reconnected with Steve Oldham, one of my old coaches. I'd known Steve for a long time, and he had played a big part in my success as a young cricketer. Developing players was his speciality, fast bowlers in particular. He'd also done well with the Yorkshire Academy side but had taken a bit of a knock when he'd brought John Blain in. I knew I was starting to tick again, and I really wanted to get back to playing at a high level, so Steve was a natural person for me to work with. After just one session with him, I felt so much more comfortable, and his understated 'Tha' looks good, lad' gave me the confidence that I was ready to play again. Losing someone like Steve when the coaching staff was gutted prior to Jason Gillespie and Paul Farbrace coming in was a big deal, because he was a big figure around the club, and he always had my back.

Cricket was all I'd ever known, and after working with Steve, I felt in a better space mentally, so I started the season for club side Sheffield United. I was performing well, and I was also training with Derbyshire. Billy Godleman, the captain at the time, was really pushing for me to be given an opportunity in the second team, but the budget can be an issue for smaller counties like Derbyshire. They already had a full squad, and they wanted to give their existing players a chance to perform before bringing in anyone else.

Then, in May 2016, I was asked to come for a training session at Headingley, with the possibility that I could make a return with Yorkshire. Despite the way things had come to an end previously, I felt I had to go. Even though I'd been unhappy at the club, I didn't really know what the problem was or what was causing me to struggle so much, and I thought it might be different this time. If it had been clearer to me that it was the racism that I had been subjected to that was affecting me so badly, I would have had to think twice about it. But, at the end of the day, beggars can't be choosers. I'd just got married and cricket was all I'd ever known, so I felt that I had to jump at any chance that presented itself.

Not long afterwards, I got a game for the second team, and within a week I was playing for the first XI and was offered a contract to the end of the year. Alex Lees was the captain of the one-day team and Jason Gillespie was the coach, which really helped, as I got on well with them both. I always thought Alex was an impressive young man. I don't know whether losing his father at a young age played a part, but he was very mature and emotionally intelligent for his age, and he was a proper leader who was willing to make difficult decisions and wasn't just a yes man.

When I rejoined the first team, Yorkshire were near the bottom of the tables in the fifty-over and T20 competitions, but we went on a massive run from there, and we got to our second ever T20 finals day. I performed well and was the joint leading wicket taker in the T20s. I also became a fully capped player. When you first join Yorkshire, you get a cap with the academy badge on it, then you move on to the second-team cap, which has a closed white rose on it. When you get your first-team cap, it has an open rose with eleven petals on it. In the more than 150-year history of the club, fewer than 200 people have received a first-team cap, and I was one of them. There was an argument that I could have got it during my first spell, as I had hit the criteria from a performance and appearance point of view, but cap number 179 was a massive moment for me, regardless.

Those two or three months were probably some of the most fun I've had playing cricket, and, again, Alex Lees and Jason Gillespie played a big part in that. I had a lot of respect for Jason in particular. One of the most impressive things about him was the way he did his post-match debriefings. He never built us up too much if we had won, and he never laid into us too much if we'd lost. When it came to a loss, he made sure to leave you feeling positive, and his criticisms were always constructive.

When I left Yorkshire in 2014, Jason had hero status at the club. He had brought through players from the second team who had been struggling and turned their careers around, and some of the lads he'd helped to develop went on to play for England. When I returned to the club, I was surprised to find that things had changed completely, and I thought the way some of the senior players treated Jason was extremely disrespectful. He'd recently lost his father in difficult circumstances and gone through a tough period, and as a result he'd made a few lifestyle changes. One of them was that he had become vegan and publicly advocated the benefits of a meat-free diet. It was a typical, small-minded Yorkshire County Cricket Club mentality that meant him demonstrating a bit of a different perspective resulted in some of the players and staff being really disrespectful towards him. Another example that comes to mind was one time when we were staying over in a hotel after an away game, and some of the boys were in the bar mimicking the way Jason did his debriefings. It was clear to me then that others at the club did not value him as highly as I did.

I remember one training session at Weetwood in particular when one of the senior players started shouting at him, and

Dizzy said, 'I've outstayed my welcome with you guys.' It was a really sad outcome. During my time out of the game, I'd seen a bit of the real world, and from the experiences I'd had, I knew he was as impressive a coach and person as you can find.

Just before he left, he gave me a big hug and said, 'I've told them that you should be the white-ball captain.' He didn't have to do that, but he believed in me, and he was a good human being above all else. The line in the media was that he left for family reasons, but within no time at all he was back coaching, first with the Papua New Guinea national side and then with Sussex, so I always wondered if there was more to it than that. It was a really sad departure for someone who is a club legend, having delivered Yorkshire back-to-back County Championships in 2014 and 2015, and blooded a number of players who went on to play for England and achieve their dreams. I think he deserved a lot better. I wasn't too worried about what it meant for me, though. Alex Lees was still the one-day captain, so I thought my position was safe – little did I know how wrong I was.

CHAPTER 9
Why Leaders Matter
(2015–18)

When Jason left in 2016, the club advertised for a new coach and interviewed a few candidates, but there was no one Martyn Moxon liked. A couple of the coaches who were interviewed wanted freedom to make their own decisions regarding the captaincy and other team matters, and that wasn't something the club was willing to give. Instead, Martyn decided to promote from within, appointing Andrew Gale as the new coach of Yorkshire County Cricket Club and Gary Ballance as captain. Straightaway, the temperature in the room went up, and it felt like déjà vu.

One incident from the 2017 season stands out in particular. It was a T20 match against Durham on 4 August. I was talking to Adil after the Durham innings, and he asked me what I thought of the score to which I replied that I thought their score was fifteen over par. It was a completely standard observation about the state of the game, but I must have been misheard because it was reported back to Andrew that I'd said Durham were fifty over par. After the match, he confronted me in front of the other players in an aggressive manner, questioning my conversation about the score and saying, 'Why are you walking around saying they have fifty too many?' That was obviously not what I'd said, and I tried to clear up the misunderstanding, but he was having none of it. I left the game with Adil, upset and worried about my position in the team.

Despite moments like this, from a cricketing point of view, 2017 was a very successful season for me. I was the joint second leading wicket taker in the country in the fifty-over competition and joint leading wicket taker for Yorkshire and in the top ten wicket takers in the country in the T20 Blast. But off the pitch it wasn't going so well. Gary Ballance was picked to play for England quite early on in the season, and Tim Bresnan took over as captain, after which I felt things got really difficult. I know several players raised concerns about him, but I was the one who paid the biggest price for doing so.

In a T20 game against Derbyshire, there was a freak incident where I knocked over the stumps at the non-striker's end by accident, something I'd never done before in my life. A no-ball was called, and the subsequent free hit went for six. In the meeting after the game, Tim shouted at me in front of the whole team, and I got the sole blame for the loss. One person being singled out like this was not what usually happened when we lost other games. For example, in a match against Lancashire, we were winning and looked to be in a good position, because it seemed like it was going to rain any second and we were ahead of the required run rate. Then Adam Lyth, one of the senior players in the team, ran down the wicket to have a big slog and got out, and we ended up tying the game. Everyone was really frustrated, but the captain and coach not only didn't say anything to Adam, they heaped praise on him. It was another example of one rule for some, another rule for me.

But I wasn't the only player struggling with Tim's attitude, and, as I mentioned, a few of us raised our concerns. I reported what I saw at the time as bullying, mentioning it to our assistant coach Richard Pyrah, and he said, 'You know what Bres is like – just try to ignore him.' I then met with Martyn Moxon and Andrew Gale at a championship game in Scarborough to talk about it. The message I received was that Tim was really struggling because he'd not really captained before. Afterwards, they spoke to Tim, and he apologised to me, which I was happy to accept and move forward. But once I'd reported not only a senior player, one who had come through the Yorkshire ranks, but also the brother-in-law of the head coach, I had a feeling that things would be very difficult for me. It also seemed to me that I was getting a reputation for being problematic, whereas white players who raised grievances were simply considered to be assertive and were not disadvantaged by coming forward. This played into the stereotypes that people of colour are emotional, angry and don't listen, and that there is something wrong with their character if they speak up to defend themselves, as if we should be grateful for the scraps that have been thrown to us.

Another of the senior players also contributed to the challenging environment in 2017. I thought Steven Patterson was disrespectful to the coaching staff and the rest of the players, and he basically got the whole dressing room fighting, which was a big issue for us in 2017. The seeds for this were sown when Gary left Steve out of the fifty-over side earlier that season. Steve was pretty vocal about his unhappiness to the coaches and management, but the way he was treated as a result was very different to someone like Tino Best, who was told by Martyn Moxon that he was going to be sent back to the Caribbean after an argument between the two.

Later that year, at a County Championship game against Surrey at The Oval, I felt my calf tightening up, so I had to come off. After the match, I was accused of faking the injury, which really upset me – I had always been nothing but professional and would never have made out that I was injured if I wasn't. I was left out of the last home game of the year, at Headingley against Warwickshire. Some of the other senior players asked Gary why I'd been dropped, and he said that I'd ruled myself out, which wasn't right. I was then with the second team the following week, so I ruled myself out of the last game of the season because of my mental health and exhaustion.

At the end of season get-together, Steve Patterson and Andrew Hodd came up to me and told me that people had been saying that I'd been faking an injury. Again, once I'd reported what I thought was bullying at the time, I knew things were going to be difficult for me, but to hear that my medical condition was being openly discussed and that people thought I'd been faking an injury really, really hurt.

Hanif Malik, who was a board member and had been brought in to oversee matters of diversity and inclusion at Yorkshire, also came up to me and Adil at the end of season dinner and said, 'I've heard lots of rumours about racism at the club.' He then mentioned Tim Bresnan, Gary Ballance and Andrew Gale. Both Adil and I said that since the new leadership had come in, we'd never felt more unwelcome. Malik then asked us whether we wanted him to say something to the board and CEO. Adil responded quickly and said, 'No, not now.' Although I said I agreed with Adil, I wasn't so sure. It was easier for him, because he was playing for England, so he was around a lot less.

It wasn't long, however, before he had cause to wish he had been more forthright about coming forward. In the winter of 2017/18, Adil was in Australia, and he was being pressurised to go on a pre-season tour with Yorkshire. He said he wanted the time off, but he was told that if he didn't go, he wouldn't be selected to play in the County Championship. During a twenty-minute phone call with Martyn Moxon, while sitting on the balcony of his hotel room in Australia, he made the decision to retire from red-ball cricket with Yorkshire. This was another example of how the management team treated players of colour differently. Adil was a senior player, with a heavy workload due to his England commitments, so it made no sense for him to go on a pre-season tour.

In the summer, when Ed Smith came in as England selector, he picked Adil for the Test team, even though he wasn't playing red-ball cricket at county level. The morning he was selected, we went into training, and Andrew Gale and Martyn Moxon walked straight past him and didn't even congratulate him – I imagine they were fuming. The CEO then criticised the decision in the media, which made Adil feel extremely isolated. Such a circumstance was unheard of. Michael Vaughan also criticised him. Other players have done the same as Adil, before and since, but their clubs haven't taken them to task in the media, and there hasn't been the same sort of outrage from ex-players and pundits. In fact, Jos Buttler was also selected for England that summer, even though he had chosen to play in the IPL rather than the County Championship, and no one seemed too bothered about that.

This episode is very similar to the moment in the run-up to the 2013 T20 World Cup when the England selector emailed Martyn Moxon about potentially putting me and Adil in the thirty-man squad, and Martyn said he shouldn't. These incidents speak to the undertone of bias in the game, as this kind of reaction would likely not have occurred if Adil or I were white.

A similar thing happened to me that winter. I was invited to play in the Cricket on Ice tournament in St Moritz in February 2018 before the season was under way – in fact, pre-season hadn't even really begun by then. The event ran from the Thursday to the Saturday, so I would have only missed one or two afternoons of training to go and play in the exhibition tournament. Although it wasn't a serious cricket competition, it was a fantastic opportunity for me, because lots of top players, past and present, took part, including Virender Sehwag and Daniel Vettori, and there were coaches of T20 franchises from all over the world in attendance. As such, I thought it would be a great shop window for me. But I wasn't allowed to go.

I couldn't believe it. It felt to me like they were stopping me from progressing in my career. Other players had been allowed to miss four or five weeks of the season to play in competitions abroad, but I wasn't allowed to miss one or two days of winter training. I understood that the St Moritz tournament was just an exhibition event, but it again suggested to me that a double standard was being applied.

This was another low moment, although I'd actually been struggling for a while. Being told I couldn't play in the St Moritz tournament was a small thing in the grand scheme of things, but on top of the early signs of my wife having a difficult pregnancy and the trials of the 2017 season, I was at a breaking point, and I genuinely thought again about taking my own life. I was in a very dark place and could have spiralled further.

In March 2018, we had our annual pre-season tour. I felt I needed to be at home looking after Faryal, who didn't have her family in the UK to support her. We were hopeful that things would improve, but the irregular heartbeat was causing us a lot of stress and worry. I told the coach and director of cricket that I wanted to stay at home, but they were adamant that I needed to go on the trip. We had a really important hospital appointment later that week, at which it became clear that there were still complications, so I told Martyn that I wouldn't be going. It wasn't taken very well. But I had to be with my wife.

I remember on the day the team was leaving, I was at Headingley training, and someone was saying that I was making out the problem with the pregnancy to be bigger than it actually was. That was very hard to take. I wasn't going to share every detail of our personal lives, but I had been up front with them, and I wasn't exaggerating how serious the situation was or the effect it was having on us. It was another example of the microaggression that was directed towards me. At different times throughout the winter, I'd been left out of training sessions and I started to feel I should have never reported what I saw as Tim's bullying behaviour.

As the 2018 season started, I was spending a lot of time at hospital. Then, around the end of April, my brother and his wife lost their unborn child at twenty weeks, which was devastating. At the funeral, the coffin was no bigger than a shoebox. It was heartbreaking for all of the family. I was in the second team at the time, and I received no meaningful care from the club. No one asked me how I was after the death of my brother's baby, and no one said, 'How's your family? How are you?'

Not long afterwards, I received a phone call from Andrew Gale in the lead-up to the first fifty-over game of the season, which was in Durham on a Friday night. Again, there was no 'How's your wife?' or anything like that. He basically just said, 'You're in the squad.' Although I'd finished the 2017 season as the joint second leading wicket taker in the country in the fifty-over competition and was in the last year of my contract,

I hadn't played much cricket in 2018 and didn't feel match fit. The main reason I didn't want to go, though, was because of everything that was going on in my private life. We were getting towards the end of the pregnancy by then, and the stress was really getting to me. But I was forced to go.

We arrived in Durham on the day before the game, and I was told that I wasn't playing. I don't think I've ever been so angry in my life. But I didn't say anything. I just kept quiet. Faryal had an important appointment on the Friday, and they knew the situation at home, and they knew they weren't going to play me, so why did they take me all the way up there?

I participated in the practice on the Thursday, and then on the day of the game, I didn't speak to the captain or coach, but I did all my twelfth-man duties in the warm-up. I was in the nets and Andrew Hodd came up to me and said, 'Have they told you why you're not playing?' And I said, 'They told me because you're in the side, they need an extra batter.' That's not what they'd told him, and it seemed to really piss him off that they hadn't been honest with us. I spent the rest of the day running on drinks, and I did a stint in the Sky commentary box for a bit, which was good fun.

When I returned home after the game, everything seemed normal. Faryal had been to the appointment on the Friday, and she felt fine, although that didn't change the fact that I thought I should have been with her and was still upset that I'd been made to travel to Durham unnecessarily. I couldn't help but think that it might have made a difference if I had been there. Perhaps I could have pushed for extra tests or spoken up when Faryal was feeling scared. Not being at the appointment is one of the biggest regrets of my life.

We spent Saturday getting ready for the arrival of our son and were feeling excited about becoming parents. Faryal's baby shower had been the week before, so there were gifts that needed to be put together, ready for the new baby. On the Sunday morning, I woke up and headed to the ground for the game against Warwickshire at Headingley. It was after the warm-ups when I was sitting on the balcony that the devastating phone call came from the hospital, and I later discovered that our unborn son Alyaan had passed away, changing everything.

Islam teaches us that after three days, you should try to get back to normal life. I understood the reason for that, even though it seemed like it would be easier said than done. But regardless of how difficult it might be, it was very important for me to try, so I decided I needed to get back to playing cricket as soon as possible after the death of my son.

Straightaway, I felt like I wasn't wanted. I messaged Andrew Gale to ask if I could train at the upcoming second-team match at York, and he said, 'You know what, why don't you play?' I replied, 'Yeah, I will do. That's brilliant.' But then ten minutes later, he messaged back to say, 'You can bowl at the mitts.' This meant I would be bowling in the warm-up but not playing, which was really weird, because he'd just said I could play. I don't know what happened in those ten minutes to change his mind.

Then, on my first day back at the club, Martyn Moxon took me into the coach's room and ripped shreds off me. He blamed me for Andrew Hodd retiring and gave me a dressing-down for not speaking to Andrew Gale and Steven Patterson at the game in Durham. He eventually reduced me to tears. At no point did he ask me how I was or how my wife was, and this was just a few days after the loss of our son. That was when I knew for sure that my time at Yorkshire was coming to an end. I'd felt since reporting Tim Bresnan for bullying and discussing racism with Hanif Malik that I was on shaky ground, but it now seemed a certainty that I was going to be pushed out. I feared my life would be made a complete and utter hell. And that's exactly what played out from there on.

The captain rang me and said he'd questioned the coach as to why I wasn't being brought back into the first team straightaway, and he'd been told that the coach didn't trust me. But I believe one of the reasons I wasn't allowed to play in that second-team game at York was because if I'd performed well, which I'm sure I would have, they'd have felt obliged to play me in the first team, who were in the quarter-finals of the fifty-over competition.

I remember someone saying something like, 'It's not fair on a young lad if we play you instead. He's travelled with us to the quarter-final.' I couldn't believe what I was hearing. It wasn't fair on a young lad who had travelled with the squad, but I'd had to travel to Durham after losing my son and not played, and missed out on playing. It made absolutely no sense.

To me, it felt like a clear case of institutional racism. The club's attitude seemed to be, 'How dare you speak up. How dare you report the coach's brother-in-law. How dare you mention racism. How dare you report bullying.' There were always going to be consequences for those actions.

As I went through the 2018 season, things became increasingly difficult for me mentally. Every time I left my house, I was really worried about Faryal, who was full of grief and anger. She'd smash things, and I eventually had to call my mother-in-law in Karachi to come over and help out. It was an extremely difficult period, but, again, I got no meaningful support from the club.

During that time, lots of people said to me, 'Don't neglect yourself,' but how could I not? I had to look after my wife and get back to some sort of normality. All the while, I knew full well that I was seriously struggling myself. So, it was a really tough period.

We started the T20 tournament in June, and although I'd set myself high standards over the years and was probably not playing as well as I had, I was still holding my own. We had a couple of days off, so I took my wife, mother-in-law and mum to London for a short visit. The first day there, we were doing some of the touristy things, and I received a message from Andrew Gale that he was leaving me out of the T20 side. We sent some messages back and forward, and I more or less said to him that he'd used everything that I'd gone through to get rid of me. He cut me off and said he didn't want to continue the conversation over text.

It spoiled our couple of days in London, and I'd had enough of the way I was being treated and the racism in the dressing room, so I arranged a meeting with Yorkshire CEO Mark Arthur for when I returned.

When I got back, I went to training the next day. I was sitting in the dressing room when Andrew Gale walked through the door, looked at me, turned around and left, and then came back with Martyn Moxon. They took me into the coach's room, and Martyn started shouting at me again: 'I've seen the messages. You don't know what Galey's gone through this year. He's found it really tough.'

I said, 'Hold on a minute, Martyn. Galey's found it tough? I've just lost my son, and you guys have treated me like shit.'

Andrew then started shouting at me at the top of his voice: 'Gary found you difficult to captain.'

I said, 'Well, let's get Gary in here then.'

And they basically just shouted at me in this tiny room, telling me all of the things I'd done wrong. And then Martyn told me to go home.

'Are you suspending me?' I asked.

'No, I just want you to go home and have your meeting with Mark and then we'll see how things stand.'

I said, 'I don't think this is right, but I'll go.' And I collected my stuff and went home.

A few days later, there was the now infamous meeting with Mark Arthur. My Professional Cricketers' Association (PCA) representative Matthew Wood, who later testified against me, was there, and my agent was supposed to come, but I had a feeling that he would pull out, because he had some personal issues he was going through at the time. Once I knew he wasn't coming, I asked my friend, the successful businessman Ritchie Fiddes who had been a sponsor at the club and knew what it was like, to come in his place. I felt it was important to take him, because we had a good relationship, and he really backed and supported me. At the same time, if I had been in the wrong, he would have told me straightaway. It turned out that Martyn Moxon had also been invited at the last minute.

Before the day of the meeting, I'd gone to see Hanif Malik, the inclusivity and diversity board member who had raised the issue of racism at the club with me and Adil Rashid in 2017. I went through all of my notes with him at his home, and I literally cried in his front room. I really expected that he would help me. And that day he did say that he would make sure that this was all sorted. I later found out when I did a data subject access request – the process by which an individual can request all personal information that an organ- isation holds about them – and through Hanif's statement that he'd gone behind my back and called the club the minute I'd walked out of his house; this surprised me as a few days after I'd met him, and after I had the meeting, he told me he was going to email Mark Arthur for the first time. I was ultimately glad that he did, as it unwittingly provided a vital piece of information. It showed that, at a time when Yorkshire were claiming they had no knowledge of my complaints, and Matthew Wood from the PCA was suggesting that I had not shared with him any of the details of the racism I had experienced, I had indeed spoken to a board member and that those concerns had been shared with the CEO. It proved that their denials held no truth.

You might have expected the PCA to have been more helpful at this time, and, to be fair, as an organisation they had been supportive in the past when the likes of Jason Ratcliffe, who was assistant CEO, and Ian Smith, who was the organisation's legal director, were involved. As soon as you had any issues, a representative would drive straight up and try to help. They offered incredible levels of support, and you felt like it was a proper union with its members' best interests at heart.

They had helped me at various points in my career, perhaps most significantly when it came to my mental health problems, and I also got into some debt because of gambling in 2017. They gave me some advice and a loan to help pay off the debt, which I subsequently repaid.

However, when it comes to the issue of racism, they have not been effective. I first raised my concerns about bullying and racism with them back in 2017, and when I asked them for legal help after speaking out, they rejected my claim after a phone call that couldn't have lasted more than about three minutes. Despite repeated requests for help from then on, especially during some of my darkest hours, I have received no real support from the organisation, which has been incredibly disappointing. They do some excellent work, but as a players' union, I just don't think they are fit for purpose. The PCA chief executive Rob Lynch accepted that the union had failed to support me in the wake of my racism allegations, and admitted they did not meet the standards they needed to.

The meeting with Mark Arthur and Martyn Moxon itself was horrific. I went through all the things that I'd written down, going over the instances of overt racism, my lack of opportunities and the way the coaches had treated me. I mentioned the people who I thought had taken issue with me, and I talked about race and bullying and how it had brought me close to taking my own life.

At one point in the meeting, Mark Arthur said, 'Where are we going with this?' And Martyn didn't look at all interested – in fact, his body language was very aggressive – and no one from the club even took any notes. But that didn't stop me pouring my heart out and getting everything off my chest. I was very clear that I needed to get this dealt with once and for all.

I later asked Ritchie what his impressions of the meeting were: 'It was an appalling meeting. They knew full well who I was: I had supported the club as a sponsor for years and met both Moxon and Arthur on numerous occasions. Arthur always greeted me by name. But on this occasion, they started by saying, "Who are you and what business do you have here?" in a completely unnecessarily hostile manner. It felt obvious to me they resented any outside presence that could expose the way they behaved.

'Azeem really opened his heart in that meeting. A couple of times, especially when he was talking about the loss of his son, he broke down in tears. He was obviously a broken man crying out for help. But Moxon just tutted, rolled his eyes and looked at the clock. The lack of basic care for a fellow human in obvious pain was diabolical. It was unprofessional, of course. But it was also rude, dismissive and completely lacking in sympathy. I was shocked by it.

'Arthur seemed out of his depth. We were in his office, but it was clear Moxon was in charge. He behaved as if he was untouchable. As if dealing with a bereaved young player was beneath him. It seemed obvious they just wanted rid of Azeem.

'At one stage, Arthur said to me, "You're experienced in business; what would you do in this situation?" I told him it was obvious: you have a full, independent investigation.'

Towards the end of the meeting, Ritchie asked, 'Has Azeem done anything wrong?' They said no and that I would be getting a new white-ball contract at the very least. And that's the way it was left. There was also an agreement that I would be able to write a statement explaining why I had not been playing as much cricket – basically because of the loss of my son. Seven days later, they got rid of me.

Martyn came to see me this time and said the club didn't have the budget to keep me. I thought that was just an excuse and this was all due to me raising my concerns about bullying and racism. It really felt like they were using the loss of my son to get rid of me, which to me is very revealing of the organisation I was dealing with. The link to the statement was not sent to the press. This is when the tirade of online abuse really became overwhelming.

I lost all faith in humanity. I passed my flat keys to my dad and said, 'We're going to Pakistan.' And I wasn't sure we would ever come back again.

CHAPTER 10
Speaking Out (August 2020)

We were in Pakistan for seven months, and when we first arrived, I genuinely thought that I didn't ever want to come back to England. But I was slowly but surely able to build myself back up. We went on a pilgrimage to Saudi Arabia, then Faryal got pregnant again, and we decided to come back to the UK in 2019. I played some minor county cricket, and I had it in the back of my mind that I wanted to find a new club, but the main priority was Faryal and the baby.

This second pregnancy was also beset with difficulties. As you can imagine, we were full of anxiety and panic that we were going to lose another child. We were in and out of the hospital for tests, and it was an extremely challenging time. We felt powerless again and didn't know what to do. But in July 2019, following an emergency birth, we had our baby boy Ayaan.

Because we wanted to make everything as different as possible from our previous experience, we decided that we would change hospital and go to the Sheffield maternity unit instead of the one in Barnsley. However, as the due date was approaching, Faryal started to bleed, and it became clear that we had to get help as quickly as possible. I didn't know what to do: stick with the decision to go to Sheffield or take Faryal to Barnsley hospital, with all of its bad memories. I felt like the pressure was on me to make the right choice, so I rang the midwife and she said we should just go to Barnsley. But for some reason, I couldn't get it out of my head that we would be better off in Sheffield, so I made a split-second decision and headed down the M1. It was rush hour, tipping it down with rain and the traffic was terrible, so I was panicking the whole way. But we got there in time.

When Ayaan arrived, it felt quite surreal to see him healthy and full of life, particularly when I thought back to what it was like when Alyaan was delivered. That trauma was still very much with me throughout the labour, whereas Faryal doesn't really remember much about what was going through her head, because of the anaesthetics. Either way, we were both full of relief and happiness and thanks that our beautiful baby boy was here safe and sound.

Around this time, I started doing Amazon deliveries. I'd go to the gym at six o'clock in the morning, then I'd go and do my Amazon driving before going back to the gym again. That was the routine I got into in preparation for a return to cricket in 2020, and I actually quite enjoyed it. There were no pressures or worries, and I could just concentrate on doing my job, getting into shape and enjoying family life.

Early in 2020, we went to Pakistan, and my grandma passed away, she had lived with us all our lives so it was a difficult time, especially for my father. Then, when we got back, Covid happened. Initially, like everyone else, I remember not really knowing what we were dealing with, then watching the news and being really scared. But as we settled into lockdown, it felt to me like an opportunity for reflection. I know that for other people it was a really terrible time, and I don't want to minimise the seriousness of the pandemic, especially as my father was very ill and considered to be vulnerable, and we had friends who worked in the NHS, but with the world suddenly shut down, I could step off the treadmill, which I felt like I'd been on for such a long time, and take a breather.

Then, in May 2020, George Floyd was murdered in Minneapolis in the USA and the Black Lives Matter cause was brought to the forefront of people's attention, with huge protests all around the world. It felt like a massive moment. Watching how the black community came together, and how other people of all races who were sympathetic to their mission rallied around them, felt like it could signal a much-needed cultural shift. It was an opportunity for people to reflect on the systemic racism in society, and it sowed the seeds for me wanting to speak out.

When Covid happened, as a family we started to take in food for NHS and other key workers. Initially, it was fruit and chocolates, then we started selling meals we'd made to raise money so that we could deliver more free meals to hospital workers. Because we knew so many people that were at the coalface of the pandemic, and because of how stressful and full-on it was for them, it was a little way of giving something back. Then, as the pandemic progressed, I turned that idea into a business called Matki Chai, selling Asian tea and Pakistani snacks. It was a lot of hard work but also really fun. And that's when Taha Hashim from *Wisden* got in touch and said he wanted to do an interview about the work I'd been doing during Covid.

In the run-up to doing the interview, I had seen that Yorkshire had put diversity logos on the sleeves of their shirts, and their hypocrisy really got to me. In the wake of the Black Lives Matter movement, a lot of sports teams added similar messages to their tops, and there was a huge debate about whether it was appropriate for sports people to take the knee to highlight their solidarity with the cause, but I felt, as a result of my experiences, that Yorkshire's gesture was purely performative and lacked substance.

Around that same time, the ex-England international Michael Carberry spoke out about his experiences of racism in cricket. This was followed by Martyn Moxon being interviewed by Chris Waters in the *Yorkshire Post* and Martyn saying that in his time in cricket he had never been around or experienced any sort of racism. I thought it was, quite frankly, tone deaf for Martyn, a middle-aged white man, to give that interview, but I also knew it wasn't true. I'd sat in his room less than two years before and talked about everything that I'd gone through. I could point to ample examples of racism within the Yorkshire dressing room, so for him to have said what he did only amplified my feelings of frustration, anger and upset.

It was not the first time that a member of the club had failed to deal properly with racist incidents. In 2003, then chairman Colin Graves refused to sanction Darren Lehmann for racist comments he had made about Sri Lankan cricketers, even though he was found guilty by the ICC. And Andrew Gale had also been banned for racist behaviour in the past, namely an incident with Ashwell Prince in 2014, although Prince later said that he had not detected any racist intention himself. Despite Gale being suspended by the ECB, Robin Smith and Martyn Moxon refused to follow suit and offered him their public backing.

Black Lives Matter and Martyn's interview provided the recent context within which the interview with Taha for *Wisden* took place. It was first and foremost an interview about my business and what I'd been doing outside of cricket during the pandemic, but towards the end Taha asked me if I had ever experienced racism in the game. I got a bit emotional and said a little bit about what I'd gone through. I talked about playing for an openly racist captain, with many people jumping to the wrong conclusion about whom I was referring to, which was itself revealing, and I also mentioned the quote made by Michael Vaughan: 'There's too many of you lot; we need to have a word about that.' But I didn't name him at the time, and he has continued to deny that he ever said it. The Squire Patton Boggs (SPB) investigation found he did say it, but most famously Vaughan was later cleared by the Cricket Discipline Commission (CDC) who found it not proven.

Although I didn't go into the interview with any intention that I was going to speak out, and nor did I have any agenda about eliciting a response from Yorkshire, I genuinely thought that when the interview was published, the club might get in touch, and we could all sit in a room and I'd be able to get some of the answers I wanted. We'd then work out a way to move forward and make sure the same thing didn't happen again. Unfortunately, Yorkshire had different ideas. It was just pin-drop silence to the *Wisden* article from the club.

Then, out of the blue, I received a message from Hanif Malik, who was still the inclusivity and diversity board member, because he wanted to have a chat about the Wisden article. I asked him if he was getting in touch in a personal capacity or as a representative of the club. He said personal but we could then make it professional if I wanted. I said, 'Look, I'm happy to chat in a personal capacity. But what I don't want is for the club to portray to the press that you have been in regular contact with me.' I had a suspicion that they would try to paint any sort of informal and infrequent contact as a sign that they had reached out to me regularly and in an official capacity.

Around that time, James Buttler, who ran the *Cricket Badger* podcast, got in touch with me and asked if I wanted to come on his show. I knew him a little bit as he'd worked at the club when I was coming through the ranks, but we hadn't spoken for a while. Looking back, I can see this as another example of Allah sending someone to look out for me. I agreed to do the podcast, and this time I shared a little bit more and described my experiences in greater detail, but without going really deep. I had gone through such a wide range of experiences and emotions, and I could only say so much on a podcast.

Again, there was no official response from Yorkshire to the interview with James, although I did speak to Hanif Malik on the phone again. He told me that Roger Hutton, the club chairman, wanted to meet with me, and he asked me if he could share the conversation he'd had with me with Mark Arthur. I reiterated that I was happy to have an informal conversation with Hanif, but, again, I didn't want them to use it as a way of making it seem like the club had reached out to me in an official capacity, which is what eventually transpired when Yorkshire subsequently said that they had been in regular contact with me. That was a stretch by any standards, but in the circumstances, it felt like deceit. It seemed to me as though Hanif had used the guise of friendship to justify his approaches and make it appear as if Yorkshire were listening.

James was also getting really frustrated with the lack of official response from Yorkshire. He'd been an employee of the club, and talking to me had made him reflect and think back to instances where he himself had seen discriminatory behaviour directly. He couldn't understand why Yorkshire weren't doing anything to address this serious problem head-on, and he just wanted his club to do better. It was at this point that he suggested I needed to get in touch with a more senior figure in the media, so he introduced me to George Dobell, who was at ESPNcricinfo at that time. James initially spoke to George when he was covering an international match and suggested that he listen to the podcast. George then got in touch with me through James. Although George was a well-known figure in the sport, and we'd probably crossed paths at a game he'd covered, I couldn't remember having spoken to him before, but he called me, and we had a good chat. While we were having that phone call, George received a message from Yorkshire saying that the inclusivity and diversity board member had been in regular contact with me. I rang Hanif Malik afterwards and said, 'Don't ever contact me again.'

In my interview with George, I shared a bit more, and I even talked about coming close to suicide. It was George's platform, his place in the game and the reach of ESPNcricinfo that broke the story into something bigger. I didn't really realise that would be the case when I spoke to him – if anything, I just thought the interest in what I had to say would grow organically, as it had done following the *Wisden* and *Cricket Badger* interviews.

Over the next few days, I was interviewed by all the big broadcasters and media outlets – the BBC, Sky, radio stations and print publications. The Sky news interview with Inzamam Rashid airing was a particularly difficult moment for me. Although I had gone into detail about my experiences in my interview with George, there was something even more powerful about talking to someone about them in front of a camera, and it felt like my story reached a much wider audience. It was also the first time my family found out about the true extent of what I'd been going through, as I'd kept from them how much I'd been struggling. I think of myself as being a bit of an extrovert, and I have a tendency to hide how I'm really feeling, putting a smile on my face and getting on with things. That probably wasn't the best thing to do, but it was my way of dealing with it.

Following the ESPNcricinfo article, I got a phone call from Tom Harrison, the CEO of the ECB at that time, and he seemed sympathetic and understanding, though I couldn't help but feel like the organisation didn't want to deal with the problem. Harrison said he couldn't get involved until after Yorkshire had finished their investigation, though he later said his board would not let him get involved. It seemed to me like the powers that be hoped things would die down and the issue would go away.

However, the sustained media coverage over the next week or so put pressure on Yorkshire to eventually launch an investigation into what had happened. They said it was independent, but they used a law firm, Squire Patton Boggs (SPB), that the chairman at the time had connections to. It invited suggestions of a conflict of interest, however Yorkshire insisted the chairman 'no longer had any connection, personal or professional, to Squire.' Yorkshire also put together what they referred to as an independent panel to adjudicate on the findings of the SPB investigation, headed by Samir Pathak, a surgeon and alleged close friend of ex-chairman Colin Graves who still had a lot of influence at the club. It also had Hanif Malik on it, which I thought was quite staggering, bearing in mind how close he was to the story, and Gulfraz Riaz from the National Asian Cricket Council. I had spoken to Gulfraz about my experiences on a number of occasions, including at an event to launch the ECB's South Asian Action Plan back in 2018, although he denies this interaction took place. Incidentally, the South Asian Action Plan event was also the day that Steve Denison, the chair of the club at that time, approached me with a smile on his face and a glass of champagne and said, 'Must be keeping you up at night.' No one had told him that we had lost our son. I had missed pre-season, but no one thought our bereavement important enough to explain why to the club's chair. Denison later told the SPB investigation that he was 'mortified' by the comment, but he never apologised to me.

Gulfraz had written an article in which he said he was going to get me justice. And I thought, 'Hold on a minute. What the hell's going on here? These are some of the people that I went to in 2018 and they didn't do anything.' I didn't want opportunistic individuals and organisations taking advantage of the situation for their own benefit, and I wanted the panel to be properly independent, so I fought for Hanif Malik and Gulfraz Riaz to be removed from it, which they were. But even then you had a surgeon managing an investigation into institutional racism. It was, I think, incredibly naive and incompetent at best, and deliberately opaque and ineffectual at worst.

My experience has shown me that institutions often have systems so convoluted and complex that they are incredibly difficult for ordinary people to navigate, and that diminishes proper accountability. The Post Office scandal is a good example of this, and it was something that I had to battle against throughout this process. Even still, with the odds stacked against me as an individual taking on large organisations, Allah has always been on my side, and the powers that be have had to accept that I was the victim of racial harassment, discrimination and bullying.

In November, it was announced that the investigation would be completed by December, which did not signal to me that they were approaching it with a due sense of importance or seriousness. I think that was mainly because they genuinely thought I would be overly emotional and make accusations without any substance that they would be able to either kick into the long grass or use their power to refute.

Leading up to my first interview with SPB, they were very respectful in their interactions with me, demonstrating how much they were willing to listen and communicate, and how open they were to me giving my account of what had happened at the club. My friends and people close to me said I shouldn't bother cooperating with them, because they would just use whatever I gave them against me, and as I have shared, the investigation didn't seem truly independent. But I was of the view that, first, I was telling the truth and had nothing to hide, and second, that I wasn't going to give them any opportunity to put this back on me. Also, if I hadn't cooperated, that would have been a way out for them.

It was as I was preparing for the process that I learned of Yorkshire cricket's history of racism and discrimination. At the 1999 World Cup, Imran Khan, the former Pakistan prime minister, raised the problem on BBC radio: 'With Yorkshire, which is flooded with Asian people, how come an Asian just doesn't find a place? It baffles me. There's got to be an element of some prejudice.' In 2004, Terry Rooney, the Labour MP for Bradford North, told the House of Commons, 'Virtually every Test player from Yorkshire started in the Bradford League. About 60 per cent of cricketers in the Bradford League are from the Indian subcontinent. Not one of them, despite their skills and abilities, has ever been adopted by the Yorkshire County Cricket Club, even at trainee level. They have gone to other counties.' Sir Vivian Richards also experienced hostility on the grounds, sharing that, 'We used to go to Yorkshire and Headingley and people used to throw banana skins and stuff like that at [us].' On another occasion, a West Indies supporter who was defending Richards was attacked, while in 1992, a pig's head was thrown into a group of Pakistan supporters. The club were embarrassed by reports of racist abuse and violence at a Test between England and Pakistan in 1996. There were somewhere around a dozen arrests with two of them specifically for 'inciting racial hatred'.

My first of two interviews was booked in for the middle of November, and my lawyer at the time put out a press release on the morning of it. It felt important to us that we got our side of the story out there. I know how uncomfortable that made SPB, but I felt all along that we had to keep the pressure on them as I was sceptical from the outset that we could trust them.

The first interview ended up taking eight hours. It was extremely difficult to go over everything in detail including the personal trauma I'd experienced, and it was made especially hard when lawyers were having to challenge me and play devil's advocate.

I had a lot of information to provide and the proof to back it up. We had of course done a data subject access request, and I was shocked by how openly my allegations and grievances were discussed in emails and other forms of club communication.

This was when I first found out that Hanif Malik had gone behind my back after I'd visited him at his house in August 2018. Five days later, he had sent me a message saying that he thought we should let Mark Arthur know that we'd met, just to be transparent, but the subject access request showed that the minute I walked out of his house, he had let Arthur know what we'd discussed. Over the course of the eight hours, I made it clear this was not something that could be glossed over.

Not long afterwards, I received legal advice that I should file a claim against the club at an employment tribunal because it would force Yorkshire to state their side of things in a public hearing, and it would make the independent investigation properly accountable. If there had been more transparency from the club and a willingness to sit down with me and work out a way forward, so that what happened to me and others could never happen again, this wouldn't have been necessary. But they didn't want to engage with me directly, and their processes suggested that they wanted to keep things behind closed doors, so going down the tribunal route was the best way of bringing things out into the open and avoiding a whitewash.

Throughout this period, I was contacting the PCA, and the ECB, and even contacts at Yorkshire, and saying, 'Let's get in a room and work this out.' I also had a word with Adil Rashid, and he tried to suggest the same thing too, but I guess they thought they had all of the power and that the institution would overcome the individual. Thankfully, that's not the way it has worked out.

However, it wasn't easy to pursue the claim. Our finances were tight, and we had to borrow money from family and friends, with one friend in particular helping to pay for the barristers. But with their help, we were able to bring the claim, and the employment tribunal was filed in December 2020.

CHAPTER 11
Lawyers and Investigations

A lot happened between being interviewed for the independent investigation in November 2020 and what should have been a landmark day for me on Friday, 10 September 2021, when, on the same morning as the England Test match versus India was called off because of an outbreak of Covid among the India players, Yorkshire decided to release a statement admitting that there was no question that I was the victim of racial harassment and bullying, and apologising to me and my family. Apologies from the ECB and PCA soon followed. On the surface, it might have seemed as though I'd eventually managed to get the outcome that I had been pushing for, but it wasn't as simple as that, even though it was the first time that Yorkshire had ever admitted that my allegations were correct.

I had originally been told that the SPB investigation would be completed by December 2020, but it took another ten months for its conclusions to be published. I had filed my case to the employment tribunal in December, and for that my team had spoken to a wide range of Yorkshire fans, ex-coaching staff, ex-players and other people who were supporting me, had been through similar experiences or could corroborate my allegations, but the majority of them were not interviewed by the investigation. This spoke volumes as to how limited the SPB investigation was. Still, at the end of the day they had no choice but to accept that I was a victim of racial harassment and bullying because the weight of evidence was overwhelmingly in my favour, whether that was board meeting minutes showing that I had raised my concerns about racism and bullying at an early stage, or the likes of Gary Ballance and Matthew Hoggard admitting that racist language was used on a regular basis in the Yorkshire dressing room.

This was an intensely hard time for me personally, and for my family and business. Very early on in the process, I received threats via my lawyers' website that I had better watch what I was saying and stop attacking Yorkshire, and that they knew where my family lived and where my businesses were.

Page Name:	Contact Us
Name:	Azeem Rafiq
Email Address:	Azeemisafuckingliar@hotmail.com
Contact Number:	Fuck you
Message:	This family owns a post office in Lundwood,barnsley. Do you want it trashed or do you want to stop abusing Yorkshire CCC. It is your choice

Yorkshire responded by saying that they would ban anyone who was involved, but, to my knowledge, that never happened.

Dealing with SPB and the chair of the panel, Samir Pathak, was also challenging, especially when they wouldn't share some of the information I requested before my second interview on 12 March 2021. I believe they wanted me to drop out of the process. This legal world was hard to navigate. It was the first time in my life that I'd needed to interact properly with lawyers. But I was very lucky to have support and guidance from trusted allies.

One of the few positive things to come from speaking out is that I have met some lovely, talented people over the last few years. I was now represented by Doughty Street Chambers, where my main barrister Paras Gorasia suggested that I have a conversation with Jennifer Robinson, who specialised in media law at the firm and had worked with some high-profile clients, including Amber Heard and Julian Assange. She was also interested in cricket, and she had done work for Imran Khan in Pakistan who is a hero of mine. I took a lot of strength from him throughout this ordeal. Jennifer and I met on a Zoom call and from the start I could tell she believed in me and the cause. She put me at ease straightaway.

After that initial call, she arranged for us to have a walk around Hyde Park with Jemima Goldsmith, who had a close connection to Pakistan through her ex-husband Imran Khan, with whom she had two children. It was a bit surreal, and I was pretty star-struck, as I'm sure anyone with Pakistani connections would have been in that situation. I spoke about some of my experiences, and Jemima shared some of her kids' experiences – on a human level, to get that type of support and understanding felt so important. That evening, Jemima was the first high-profile person to get behind me publicly when she posted a message on Twitter. I know a lot of people tried to divert her away from supporting me, but she refused, and I'll be eternally grateful for her backing.

From then on, Jennifer became a friend as well as a trusted confidante, and she put a huge amount of work into my case. She was in Australia during Covid, but she was in contact with me all the time, and when we were doing my witness statement, she worked on it for what seemed like twenty-four hours a day for four days straight, to make sure that it was as robust as it could be. That's the level of commitment she put into my case. In fact, her hard work on my behalf, and the belief she had in me, helped to restore my faith that there are good people out there.

Another ally was Mark Leftly from Powerscourt communication agency, who was introduced into the team by Jennifer to help advise me when it came to my dealings with the media. They'd worked together on the Amber Heard case. Mark was a massive cricket fan, and all he wanted in return for helping me out was a signed Jimmy Anderson ball, which I still haven't been able to get for him, but I hopefully will one day. He was a real support on a personal level, because I found these months really challenging mentally and was in some pretty dark places at times.

At the beginning, every single call I had with my lawyers and advisers ended up with me breaking down emotionally. I was having to go through all of my experiences time and time again, and it was incredibly raw. I found it extremely difficult to talk about, as it was so traumatic. It opened up a lot of old wounds, but I just felt like I had to share everything.

When Mark came on board, one of the main things he wanted to do was approach Michael Atherton, which he attempted, to no avail. He never replied or spoke on the situation, and I felt he showed little to no understanding. Mark was previously a political journalist and adviser, and he brought a lot of political knowledge that I didn't have myself. He said that if no one was willing to listen to me, we could always write to the DCMS select committee. Because he was working for me pro bono I just thought this would never happen as it would require more time than he had available to me. I didn't really know what the DCMS select committee was, but he was right, that was where we had to go. It was invaluable to have someone with his experience advising me, as someone who could get select committees and politicians to sit up and take notice. It wasn't until I was in front of the DCMS that I really had my voice heard.

On 30 November 2020, our baby girl Mirha was born, so it was a pretty full-on and overwhelming time, even before taking the investigation into consideration. That's why it was so helpful to have support from someone like Mark, who could help me to understand and process what was going on. Whether it was late at night or early in the morning, he made himself available if I needed someone to speak to.

A lot was happening in that period, including more back and forth with SPB and the employment tribunal. To begin with, Yorkshire tried to get my claim dismissed on a technicality. They argued that because I'd started the process more than three months after leaving the club, I was outside the statutory time limit and shouldn't be allowed to continue. I had to undergo an assessment by a psychiatrist in order to show that my mental health had been such that I couldn't have brought the claim any sooner. I also made the point that I wasn't in a financial position to bring the claim sooner and emphasised that there was a public interest element to the case. However, before we got to a hearing, Yorkshire instead suggested we go to mediation.

The mediation process between me and Yorkshire took place over two difficult days in June 2021. Prior to that, I'd been very clear that for me, speaking out was very much about the cause, and I just wanted an end to the legal side of things. However, when Yorkshire got in touch about turning to mediation, it suddenly all became about settlements, which I wasn't very comfortable with. It was not something I enjoyed being part of.

On the morning of the mediation meeting, I spoke to my lawyers and they asked me what I wanted from the process. My response was that I wanted an apology; an understanding of how we would make sure that this didn't happen again; conversations with the individuals who had put me through this; for my lawyers to be paid; and no NDAs. More than anything I wanted to be completely honest and resolve things.

The meeting was conducted over Zoom and was attended by the Yorkshire lawyers and barristers and the head of HR at the club. Unfortunately, we weren't able to resolve matters. I also remember at one point during the process I was told that if I didn't sign the settlement, I could incur all the legal bills up to date. That really opened my eyes to the challenges of fighting an institution like Yorkshire County Cricket Club. I made it very clear that I would not be signing my life off to anything, even if it would cost me. It wasn't until Lord Patel came in as the new chair of the club in November 2021 that we were finally able to come to an agreement.

He rang me on the Friday after he was appointed and asked if we could meet up on the Sunday. He wanted it to be somewhere nice and quiet, so I chose the Holiday Inn in Dodworth in Barnsley. I thought there'd be no one there on a Sunday morning. Not long after we arrived, a big group of people who had been on some sort of run or walk came in, including none other than Dickie Bird, the legendary umpire who had served as the club's president from 2014 to 2016.

You couldn't make it up. I was a bit agitated, but Dickie came over, and he was lovely.

Lord Patel and I ended up speaking for nearly six hours. But, to be honest, I disagreed with most of what he said. He said that he would go through the evidence himself and make sure everything was done properly. He thought that process would take approximately six months, after which he would ensure the right people were held accountable. I didn't agree with that approach, but we talked everything through and built up a level of respect. I explained that I wanted to know how things were going to change, and that I would both challenge and support the club until that happened. I also said that as long as the club's intentions were good, I was happy to agree to a settlement. The only other things I asked for were a donation to a charity of my choice and the creation of a bursary for underprivileged children. To this day, a donation has been made to a charity but to my knowledge, there is no bursary, even though they agreed to take reasonable steps to set one up.

On 9 May 2021 I received an email from Yorkshire's lawyers to say that Robin Smith, the chairman at the time of my allegations internally, had some handwritten notes from a meeting of senior figures at the club that had taken place on 29 August 2018. These notes were significant and would have had an impact if discovered previously. They vindicated what I'd said had happened and showed that I'd raised my concerns on multiple occasions. These notes also showed that leadership were made aware that Adil Rashid had raised concerns about the treatment of certain individuals based on race.

At the same time, the notes do not express concern for my well-being or show that my attempts to shine a light on the problem at the club were being listened to. The language is very much about ticking this box and that box, and if there were any recommendations arising from an inquiry investigation, it was that the club would put a training course together. In other words, I felt the notes were an example of the lip service around the problem of institutional racism at Yorkshire County Cricket Club.

It wasn't a surprise. Smith had been vocal about his refusal to accept that the club had been institutionally racist. This was also nothing new. When local MP Terry Rooney and some of his constituents accused the club of racism in 2004, Smith asked Ismail Dawood, as a person of colour, to speak to Rooney and deny that there was any racism at Yorkshire County Cricket Club. Dawood agreed because he didn't want to rock the boat or damage his future playing prospects. He later said that the club had taken advantage of him in order to 'discredit the pain and suffering of fellow BAME individuals'.

There was a lot of waiting I had to do in 2021. Waiting for justice and recognition, for accountability and resolution. I had given my evidence, now it was on Yorkshire to act. After having our baby girl, we wanted to take her and our son to Pakistan to see their grandparents, but I kept being told by my team not to go, in case anything happened that needed my presence. There were so many moving parts, and it felt like a 24/7 job. However, by August 2021, I was really fed up of all the waiting, so we decided just to go. On our first day in Pakistan, Yorkshire released a statement saying that I had been the victim of 'inappropriate behaviour'. I spent the day locked in a room doing media interviews, and I was so angry and drained. To minimise racism by calling it inappropriate behaviour was unacceptable. The chairman Roger Hutton was clearly in a difficult position. Around that time, he rang me and said he wanted to meet, but I didn't feel like I could fully trust him. In the past, he'd attended members' forums and said that no one at the club had been involved in any racist behaviour, which didn't inspire confidence in me now.

I did a series of interviews that day, and in them you can tell I'm pretty broken – I was very emotional, and the whole process was extremely tiring. Not long before, Ben Stokes had announced that he was taking a break from cricket to work on his mental health, and he had, quite rightly, been supported in this decision. I was asked in one of the interviews what I thought about this, so I said that my experience had been very different and that the mental health support that you receive in cricket was clearly dependent on the colour of your skin.

Not long after their first statement, in response to the summarised version of the SPB report being released, Yorkshire finally admitted that I had been the victim of racial harassment and bullying in September 2021. And I think it was about this time that the cricket world really began to sit up and take notice of what was going on. But, scarily, even having made their admission, Yorkshire nearly got away with it. Only a few weeks later, they announced that no one at the club needed to be held responsible or accountable, and things would go on more or less as they had done before.

I wasn't surprised that this was their approach. At every stage, I felt as though the institution had tried to deflect and defuse the situation so that their culpability was minimised. There was a constant lack of transparency, and the powers that be had an old-school approach when it came to dealing with these kinds of things. But this is how these things have always been dealt with, and nothing has ever changed. That's why I'm so determined to keep calling it out. A continual cycle of outrage followed by calls to move on does not result in change.

Moving on suggests forgetting about what has happened, but you can't just forget. I would rather move forward together in a sustainable way. To do that there needs to be accountability for what has happened in the past. I understand that accountability can be uncomfortable, but it is so important, because without it there is no signal to people that there are consequences if they step out of line.

So, to say I was frustrated and disappointed with Yorkshire's response is an understatement. However, we kept the pressure on, and over the next couple of months things really changed, and most people had no choice but to accept that Yorkshire County Cricket Club, and the world of cricket more generally, had been institutionally racist.

CHAPTER 12
Paki as Banter

I really wanted Yorkshire to send me the complete SPB report, but instead I received a heavily redacted version, which has still never been published. I found it quite staggering that they weren't willing to give me a copy of their findings in full, and that they thought I would just leave it there. There was nothing short of the full report that they could have provided to me that would have made me just leave it. I'd put myself through the absolute mill in an attempt to reveal the truth, and the least I deserved was full understanding of how they'd come to their conclusions.

Despite the gaps, seeing how they'd reached some of their decisions was interesting, to say the least. In particular, on Monday, 1 November 2021, an article on ESPNcricinfo revealed that the panel had come to the conclusion that 'Paki' had been used as banter in the Yorkshire dressing room. And that was it – my world changed as a result of that article being published. The funny thing is, there were other parts of the SPB report that were even more damning and would have caused more of a stir if they had been released.

Things really heated up when Sajid Javid, who was the Health Secretary at the time, tweeted: 'Paki is not banter. Heads should roll at Yorkshire CCC. If @ECB_cricket doesn't take action, it's not fit for purpose.' It was chaos after that, and for the next two months or so, we were living under the most intense scrutiny and feeling really fearful about what might happen to us.

A lot of the abuse I received was online, especially on the Yorkshire cricket forum, something that I highlighted in a couple of tweets. These types of incidents kept happening, and I remember raising them with the new board, but there was no will to actually do anything. To me, this again revealed what Yorkshire County Cricket Club really stands for, and, for that matter, what the sport of cricket at large stands for.

But the abuse wasn't confined to the online world. I owned a fish-and-chip shop that was attacked several times. One time, a man ran into the shop and started throwing food about, saying that I had a bomb and that I was a terrorist. Incidents like this put me, my family and my staff under physical threat and danger, as it just takes one person to go too far.

On another occasion, a man was outside the shop shouting and swearing and directing racially aggravated abuse at me. This was one time the police did act. The man in question was identified and arrested. I had the option to either take it further or he could explain himself and apologise, which is what he did. It was the bare minimum, but I'd already had a lot of dealings with the police, and I didn't have the energy to take it any further.

Then there was the time when someone with what looked like a chain in their hand was circling my house late at night. It was really scary, and I began to sleep with a cricket bat next to my bed. I was so anxious of any bit of movement around the house, or any unusual noise. One night, at three in the morning, I heard a car repeatedly going up and down the street, so I looked out of the window, and I just fell to the bed shaking.

Incidents like these made me fearful and a bit paranoid about what could happen. The psychological impact of being scared and constantly fearing for your safety is immense. I remember feeling petrified to even walk down the street. Around the time of the first select committee appearance, when I was in the news a lot, I went into town and this group of people started shouting things at me like, 'You fucking Paki bastard!', 'Leave the country!', 'Get out of here!' It was shocking and upsetting that people were willing to say such things to my face. Not long after I spoke out, I went into Asda, and people were giving me abuse in the store. I'd never experienced that before, and it was really scary.

I found myself in a pretty dark place. There was one day in particular, not long after my daughter was born, that gives me shivers just to think about it. I had Mirha in my arms, and I was walking down the street when I had an urge to jump in front of a car with her. That moment terrified me and showed me just how fragile I was feeling and how low I'd sunk. I went home, gave Mirha to her mum and locked myself in the toilet. During this time, when I felt really scared, I often hid myself in the bathroom. It was the only place I felt safe.

In response to the latest revelations and the intervention of people such as Sajid Javid, sponsors started to leave the club all in a rush. People rang me up and said that they thought I must be really pleased about this. But I told them, and my team as well, that I wasn't, as I didn't think it would necessarily help. Yes, it might put more pressure on Yorkshire to behave properly and be held accountable, but it was still my club, and I felt a sense of sadness that it had got to that point. Some of the sponsors had come on board after I'd spoken out, so they'd entered their partnerships with their eyes open, and I had less sympathy for them, but overall I would rather all of the sponsors had actively tried to hold Yorkshire accountable and promote change, as opposed to looking the other way and then running a mile when it got embarrassing. I would encourage brands to put processes in place with the organisations they support so that they can make a much more positive and impactful difference, and use their standing a lot earlier, when there are problems that need to be addressed.

Before that, on the afternoon of 1 November, I was asked if I would give evidence to the Department for Culture, Media and Sport (DCMS) select committee. To be honest, I didn't really know what a select committee was. I'd heard of one, of course, as Mark Leftly had mentioned them to me, but I still didn't have a good understanding of what they did or how significant it was to be asked to appear before one. Even so, I had nothing to hide, and I was absolutely happy to tell them what I'd been through. The truth was on my side, something I'd been confident of since the moment I'd spoken out.

On 5 November 2021, my representatives received an email and a phone call from West Yorkshire Police to say that they had been aware of and following my case for some time, although not in any official capacity. However, with it being in the news over the last forty-eight hours, the officers in question had been asked by their superiors to contact me and see if I would be willing to provide an account of my experiences, so that they could judge if the criteria had been met for a racially aggravated public order offence during my time at Yorkshire. They also wanted to know if I wanted them to press charges. There was a hell of a lot going on at that time, so I decided to stay in touch with the police via my representatives, with a view to me speaking to them later if I wanted to.

The days and weeks following the DCMS select committee were very challenging, so it wasn't until the new year that we decided to touch base with the police again. However, it still wasn't really a path I felt comfortable going down. One, I'd already been through a lot. And two, my trust in the police was pretty low. Well, my trust in anyone was pretty low by then, but I thought the police had been unhelpful up to this point, and in some respects had even added to the trauma that my family and I had experienced. Nonetheless, we agreed to stay in touch, and if I changed my mind, it was something I could go back to.

As the year progressed and the abuse continued, whether that was threats I received directly or ones that were being relayed to me by others, I was fearing more and more for my life and for my family's lives. The online abuse and threats were ramping up in particular, and it got to the point where I had to take that next move and get back in touch with West Yorkshire Police. I met with them and went through what had been going on and what I wanted to happen, and they were very supportive. They still needed a lot more information, but it was made clear to me that if I wanted to pursue things further, I could have gone down a criminal road. Again, I decided that was not something I wanted at that time.

One good thing that came out of that meeting, though, was that the officer I spoke to was able to contact Yorkshire County Cricket Club and speak informally to the club. I think that might have helped in terms of getting Gary and I together. Prior to this, I had been told on a number of occasions by Darren Gough that Gary wanted to meet with me so he could apologise, but nothing had ever come of it. I think maybe the police being involved, albeit in an informal capacity, spurred Gary and others on to start putting their words into action and build some bridges. That wasn't my intention – I was only interested in protecting my family – but the police taking my concerns seriously might have made all those people who were sitting on the sidelines, trying to peddle the narrative that nothing had happened and I'd blown things completely out of proportion, think twice.

I had fifteen days to prepare for the select committee, and my team briefed me a little bit on what I should expect, but it was very important to me that I went there and spoke from the heart and represented my authentic self.

My brother and I dropped my car off in Leicester the day before the hearing, and a friend who was incredibly supportive throughout this period drove us to London. First stop was the Powerscourt office. I hadn't actually met anyone there in person yet, as all of our communication had been over Zoom, so it was good to meet them in the flesh. We had a little get-together and a chat, and I got a bit emotional when I thanked them for all of their help.

Baroness Morgan, who had been the Secretary of State for Digital, Culture, Media and Sport, had also been a big support. Mark Leftly had worked with her previously, so he'd put us in touch, and I'd had a Zoom call with her in the summer in which I'd gone through all my evidence. In response, she wrote to YCCC asking for the SPB report to be published. I don't know if she knows how much of an effect she had on me, but she came into the Powerscourt offices and said, 'Just go be you. I know you. I believe you. Go tell your truth.' And that really calmed my nerves. The feeling of banging my head against the wall and not being believed, despite all of the evidence, was incredibly draining and dispiriting, so to have someone of Baroness Morgan's stature say that she believed me was a huge boost to my confidence. It's especially encouraging when someone like this backs you, even though there is no benefit to them of doing so.

That evening the late Enam Ali, who set up the British Curry Awards, took me, my brother and Mark Leftly out for a nice dinner at a Michelin-starred restaurant. It was a bit of a weird experience for me. I'm a boy from the streets of Karachi brought up in Barnsley, and there were things on the menu that I'd never even heard of before. When the food arrived, it was beautifully presented, but some of the dishes were smaller than one of my fingers. It was so funny, and my brother and I laughed and joked about it on the way back to our hotel, which was a tiny little place with rooms so small you could barely turn around in them. I spoke to the family, prayed and then went to bed, hoping to get a good night's sleep, ready for a big day in front of the committee.

After a fitful night, I woke up very early and put the news on, only to find my face looking back at me. In fact, during that period, it sometimes felt like my story was the only news in town.

We headed down to Portcullis House and met the clerk and had some coffee, with lots of MPs I recognised from TV passing by, which felt quite surreal. The clerk then took us to the committee room. I don't remember feeling nervous as such – I just felt like it was an opportunity to share and unburden myself of everything that I'd been carrying on my shoulders for such a long time.

The next hour and forty-five minutes changed my life. I was aware that there was coverage of my case, of course – I had seen myself on the news that morning, for goodness' sake – but I didn't really have any understanding of the true level of interest, and things only snowballed from that point onwards.

I had been encouraged to make some notes and read from them in case I forgot or missed anything, but I instead decided that I would just speak from the heart and answer any questions as openly and honestly as I could. My evidence was first, and to this day, I've not been able to watch it back in its entirety, although I hope I can get to a point where I can. It felt as though the eyes of the world were watching me as I sat in that room in front of all those MPs, but, again, I wasn't particularly nervous. Instead, I was quite emotional to begin with. There was a question early on about the loss of my son, and I choked up and started to cry, so they gave me a little break. Once we got going again, I've been told that I was very calm, collected, balanced and straight, which I'm pleased about, as I wanted to get it all out there and say it as I saw it.

It's difficult to remember exactly what I said, especially as I've not been able to watch the whole thing back, but there are a couple of moments that do stand out. One was when Julie Elliott, the MP for Sunderland Central, responded to me sharing my fear that I didn't really think anyone would believe me, by saying, 'Can I just say that I believe you, and I am sure this committee believes you. Do not for a second think that we do not believe you. I think most decent people in this country believe you.' To have someone in her position say that to me was huge.

The other thing that stands out, perhaps because it was another moment at which I felt extremely emotional, was when John Nicolson, MP for Ochil and South Perthshire, asked me how my cricket career had been impacted by the racism I had suffered. I suppose I should have been ready for a question like that, but it caught me a bit off guard. Deep down, I knew I had lost my career because of racism, but saying so in that moment really brought the reality home to me.

I was supposed to be in front of the committee for forty-five minutes, but, as I said, it ended up being an hour and for-ty-five. Remember, my first SPB interview was eight hours, so what I was able to say was only really a snippet of my experiences.

When I was finished, we watched the rest of the proceedings in an office provided to us by the MP Nav Mishra. Initially, Yorkshire had said they were going to send a number of representatives, but that had quickly changed. The chairman Roger Hutton, who had resigned on 5 November as a result of his disappointment with the way the rest of the Yorkshire leadership team had dealt with my allegations, was the only one who gave evidence, and the rest of the senior management team all pulled out, which didn't surprise me. Despite what the press might have written at times, Yorkshire County Cricket Club and the individuals concerned have had ample opportunities to come forward and plainly and openly put forward their side of the story, but the vast majority have not turned up and given evidence at any point. And there's a reason for that.

I think listening to Roger testify was the most difficult part of the hearing. It was the first time I found out that the terms of reference of the SPB investigation had been changed by the panel, removing their remit to investigate institutional racism. To me, this embodied everything that was wrong with the investigation and only reinforced my suspicion that it was rigged from the outset to be in Yorkshire's favour. It seemed to me like they'd put a brown man at the head of it so as to appear diverse, but that didn't equate to independence. Unfortunately for them, I wasn't easily deterred. In some ways I was a broken person, and I didn't worry about what the consequences of speaking out would be for me. I just thought it was important to have my voice heard.

When Tom Harrison and the other executives from the ECB gave their evidence, it was like watching a car crash. They'd apparently been trained to deal with these sorts of scenarios, but they did not perform at all well. It made me realise that we put a lot of our leaders on pedestals, but they are often no more qualified than you or me. I found it quite disturbing how inept and out of their depth they were. They knew they were on the wrong side, but they didn't have the humility to be straight and honest about it.

That evening, my friend came down from Leicester and we had a nice German doner kebab. It was a small thing but it was the support I needed. I also felt the same support from my family. When I first spoke out, my dad broke down before saying in Urdu, 'I have watched my son cry with blood tears.' That crushed me at the time but after it became my strength. He was there for me throughout. The next day, I went on a massive media blitz. I think I was initially supposed to do five interviews, but we found it really difficult to say no, and we ended up running around London from studio to studio. All told, I must have done more like fifteen different interviews. It was an exhausting but important day. I met some good people along the way, and I was even offered some work at a radio station, which would have been lovely, but nothing came of it.

One of the things I found most confusing was how surprised white people were about my experience. For people of colour, this is often our everyday life, and we are consistently having to defend our place in the world, navigating being racially profiled or reckoning with not getting equal opportunities. There were Black, Asian and ethnic minority people from all walks of life sharing with me their experiences during this time. For example, Dal Babu, former Chief Superintendent in the Metropolitan Police shared how 'he could count on the fingers of one hand the number of people who *didn't* use the N-word or P-word.' There was also Jahid Ahmed, former Essex cricketer, Dr Deepti Gurdasani, doctor and academic, and

Peter Herbert, barrister and judge, all of whom experienced institutional racism and regular abuse.

This was a time of connection, and my relationship with the media and social media during this time was fraught. I would get abusive DMs telling me to leave the country, but I would get other ones that would be positive and supportive. Twitter, in many ways, kept my story alive. For all those months when nothing moved and nobody listened, it was the only way I could remind people that I was still there and I wasn't going away.

The downsides, though, were significant. I read everything – everything – people said about me and the case. I ended up replying to accounts with zero followers, accounts that had clearly been set up by unhinged people who just wanted to abuse and harass me. But so zealous was I in my determination to refute every lie and injustice that I couldn't even let their comments go. I was glued to my phone. Even in the middle of the night, I would feel I had to check things. And then, infuriated by the latest lie, I would become so upset I couldn't go back to sleep. It affected my health and mood. More importantly, it affected family life. I might have been with them physically, but my family rarely had my full attention mentally. I'm really sorry about that. I saw it as a point of pride not to block anyone (blocking someone means they can no longer see your comments or interact with you) and instead resolved to make them run from me. This is something I have had to learn to stop doing.

During the long media round I was on London Bridge doing one of the interviews when I received a phone call from Wasim Khan, the CEO of Leicestershire at that time and the highest-profile South Asian administrator in the country. I'd first met him back in 2018 at the South Asian Action Plan, and I'd told him then a little bit about what I'd been through.

I wish he would have helped but that didn't happen, so I mentioned this during my evidence to the select committee. After seeing me raise this, he called to offer one of the most authentic and genuine apologies I have received during this process. He was in tears and spoke about certain moments in his playing days. It meant the world to me that he reached out, and he has subsequently played a huge part in helping me move forward with my life.

Another person who got in touch with me after my DCMS appearance was David 'Bumble' Lloyd. After I'd come forward about my experiences, it had transpired that he'd been speaking to anyone who would listen about his views on the issues I'd raised and what he thought about me. The thing was, he didn't know me, so his opinions must have come from somewhere in the first place. Regardless, he was a powerful figure in the game, so I thought him briefing against me was wrong. He wasn't the only one, of course, although no one did it so openly and in writing.

That's why I mentioned him during the DCMS hearing, saying that he had been spreading rumours about me. He admitted to the text message exchange with me where he questioned my personal life and the Asian community's willingness to participate in the social side of club cricket. He later apologised to me and said 'I deeply regret my actions' in a tweet he posted. I was happy to accept his apology at the time.

Since then, David lost his role at Sky which I felt was the wrong thing, and the cricket world has painted him as a victim. However, since his apology to me, he has contacted at least one person privately to discredit my experience further. Sadly, I don't think any lessons have been learned and I believe he could have used his power and influence for good to change the game for the better.

We have to take a more sophisticated approach to such errors. We have to acknowledge that perfection isn't a human quality, and that by simply cancelling someone we are denying their ability to learn and grow. We are also preventing an opportunity for connection and consolation. Such intolerance will only lead to more trenchant refusals to admit wrongdoing, and more anger and ignorance. It will create more divides and result in a less honest, more narrow-minded society.

After completing my media interviews, I felt happy that it had all gone well and that I had given a good account of myself. However, the very next day, late morning or early afternoon, old anti-Semitic comments that I'd regrettably made surfaced, threatening to undermine all of my hard work and progress.

CHAPTER 13

Accountability

In the days following my appearance in front of the DCMS select committee, I was the victim of many attempted smears. There were stories of theft, of violence, of sexual impropriety and a million other things. They were all rubbish.

This wasn't like that. When news broke of anti-Semitic posts I had made on social media a decade earlier, it wasn't a smear. It was me quite rightly being held accountable for my own ignorance. I was 100 per cent guilty, and I will, to my dying day, be ashamed of what I wrote and the pain I caused. It was foul, it was hurtful, it was damaging and it was wrong. I am very sorry.

I didn't remember the exchange, which dated back to 2011. I was nineteen at the time – plenty old enough to know better – and was talking to my England Under-19s teammate Ateeq Javid. But it was me.

The first I knew of it was a phone call from Mark Leftly from Powerscourt. As I've mentioned, Mark treated me really well. The time and patience he extended towards me were incredible. But on this occasion, he could barely contain his anger and disappointment. He started by asking me whether it was true and then asked me what I really thought on the subject. I told him I didn't remember the posts, but, upon checking, it was clearly me, and it obviously didn't matter if I could remember them or not – they were unacceptable. I also told him I was sorry. I told him that though this would be horrible for me, which was what I deserved, it did highlight how big the problem was.

The first thing to do was apologise. I didn't want any qualification or caveats or whataboutery in it. I didn't want any of that mealy-mouthed stuff about 'sorry to anyone who might be offended'. I wanted to take responsibility. I wanted to admit fault. I said all of this to Mark, who wrote it down and said, 'Right, that's your statement.' I then posted it on Twitter:

> I was sent an image of this exchange from early 2011 today. I have gone back to check my account and it is me – I have absolutely no excuses. I am ashamed of this exchange and have now deleted it so as not to cause further offence. I was nineteen at the time and I hope and believe I am a different person today. I am incredibly angry at myself and I apologise to the Jewish community and everyone who is rightly offended by this. That evening, Marie van der Zyl, president of the Board of Deputies of British Jews, released a statement saying, 'Azeem Rafiq has suffered terribly at the hands of racists in cricket so he will well understand the hurt this exchange will cause to Jews who have supported him. His apology certainly seems heartfelt and we have no reason to believe he is not completely sincere.'

I took a similar approach when it became apparent that the ECB were going to charge me for bringing the game into disrepute as a result of the posts. I told the ECB very early on that I would plead guilty to the charge, and that I was happy for everything to be made public. It's what I deserved, and it's the only way justice could be done and be seen to be done.

I was acutely aware of all the people I had let down. All the people who had supported me; all the people who had stuck their heads above the parapet to fight my case. I had a series of uncomfortable conversations with Mark, George Dobell and James Buttler in particular, in which I said I would understand it if they could no longer support me. Although angry and disappointed, they were all more understanding than I had any right to expect.

I was gutted to learn how many Jewish people had supported me during my career, and when I spoke out. I called Alex Sobel, the Member of Parliament for Leeds North West, who had supported my cause without me even knowing by sending several letters to the club and has continued to show brave leadership to this day at a time when most leaders have looked the other way. I called Dave Rich, who is Head of Policy at the Community Security Trust, an organisation that provides security advice to the Jewish community. I called Lord John Mann, who serves as an adviser to the government on anti-Semitism, and I called Jack Mendel, who was a journalist at *Jewish News*. All of them were unimpressed. But all of them listened.

Then an amazing thing happened. Instead of ostracising me or criticising me, the Jewish community opened its arms and offered to educate me. I was invited, first of all, to the Jewish Museum in London. There I learned why my comments had reinforced damaging racial stereotypes. I learned about the context and connotations of what I'd said.

I met Ruth, a survivor of the *Kindertransport*, the rescue effort which took children from Nazi-controlled areas to safety, as war clouds gathered ahead of the Second World War. I heard how she was separated from her parents, aged four, and

133

how, having struggled to forgive them, she then struggled to forgive herself for judging them so harshly.

I went to a synagogue in London where I met Lily Ebert. Along with her mother, brother and three sisters, she was sent to Auschwitz-Birkenau in 1944. And while her mother, brother and younger sister were immediately sent to the gas chamber, she survived. She went on to raise a family and, during the Covid pandemic, wrote a book, *Lily's Promise*, which tells her story and educates people about what happened. I will never forget the moment she rolled up her sleeve to show me the tattoo by which the Nazis had identified her in Auschwitz.

It's embarrassing to admit, but I had never heard of the Holocaust. That might seem shocking, but I'm being honest. Knowing what I know now, I appreciate this is hardly credible. But it's true. I'd heard the name 'Hitler', but I didn't know much more than that, and I wouldn't have known the dates of the World Wars within a hundred years.

I can only blame myself for this ignorance. I went to school; I had access to TV and the internet. But I guess I was so wrapped up in myself, in playing cricket, that I didn't allow any of this information inside my head. If you wanted to know where to place your mid-on or extra cover, I was brilliant. But if you wanted a basic overview of history, geography or politics, I was deeply and shamefully ignorant. Perhaps this is also why I could initially let the names I was called wash over me. I didn't quite understand where they came from, or the hurt they inflicted.

I'm a little bit less ignorant now. Through the generosity of spirit I encountered from the Jewish community, I learned about Anne Frank, and I visited Auschwitz. I have learned how little I knew, how far the evils of discrimination can lead, and how important it is to understand history to appreciate what can happen if ignorance and hate are allowed to fester.

Very often, these invitations were humbling. How did it come to pass, I have often thought, that an off-spinner from Yorkshire should find himself standing next to Queen Camilla, the Duchess of Cornwall as she was at the time, having been invited to be one of five candle lighters asked to commemorate the seventy-fifth anniversary of the publication of Anne Frank's diary on Holocaust Memorial Day? It was an emotional experience. Mark had written an introduction for me that was read out by the announcer before I lit my candle. It was clear Mark was still angry with me, and that he felt there should be no excuses made for my anti-Semitic comments. The description of me and of what I'd done was excruciating. But I deserved it, and it served to show how far I had come and how much I still had to learn. It was a massive honour to be invited that day.

It also led to the visit to Auschwitz. I was asked during an interview with ITV whether I would consider going, and I said I would. March of the Living, an education programme which encourages trips to Poland to learn about the Holocaust, had already been in touch to offer just such a trip. I jumped at the chance.

In many ways, though, I hadn't thought it through. We made the trip in the last week of Ramadan, so my sister Amna, who came along with me, and I were both fasting. But the support we received was incredible. One night, a rabbi brought us dates so we could break our fast. Another night, the entire travelling party waited to eat so we could break fast together. Not for the first time, I was humbled by the generosity of spirit the Jewish community extended towards me.

We were on an interfaith bus, which was the most incredible experience. I made friendships for life with people from all religions. Every bus had a Holocaust survivor on it. On ours was a ninety-one-year-old lady called Agnes Kaposi, and she was one of the most amazing human beings I've ever met. She went on the mic, and it was such an inspiration to listen to someone who had been through so much, but had then been able to rebuild her life, and rebuild it in such a positive manner.

As well as being inspirational, the trip was also shocking and draining. We watched *Schindler's List*, Steven Spielberg's incredible film about the German industrialist who tried to save his Jewish employees during the Holocaust. It was the first time I had seen it. At Auschwitz, we went into one building that was filled with hair taken from women. We went into another piled with clothes. A pair of baby shoes caught my eye and made me think about my own kids and the almost unfathomable cruelty that had taken place there.

There was also a room where the names of everyone who had lost their lives was written in a large book. Our bus leader had only recently found out that her family was murdered there, and it was extremely emotional listening to her talk about when she'd found out and watching her go through the book to look for the names of her family members. Although it was an incredibly difficult moment, I think it's important to understand history so we can learn from it.

In total, there were seven survivors who made the trip with us. To listen to one of them talking outside the barracks where his family were murdered will stay with me for ever. As will the sight of the hotel in Lublin, originally built as a Jewish centre of study, but now housing Ukrainian refugees who had nowhere else to go. Sometimes it seems we haven't learned very much. As I asked often on the trip, 'Where was everyone? Why didn't anyone intervene? How was this allowed to happen?'

On the last day, there was a big event, and a survivor who was not on the trip spoke to us. I could see the trauma that they had been through. Agnes had been able to move forward with her life, at least outwardly, but this Holocaust survivor was really struggling. What that told me is that everyone's on a journey. People take different times to get to where they need to go, and to feel at ease with the things that happen in their lives. It's really important to understand that.

The reaction of the Jewish community has also taught me a great deal. It has provided a model of forgiveness and education, and shown that we are capable of taking negative experiences and turning them into positive ones. I remain humbled and grateful for the patience they have shown towards me. I won't forget it, and I take the responsibility for putting the lessons I've learned into action seriously.

What I didn't feel, at any stage, was that my own transgressions undermined the overall message I was trying to spread. Yes, they showed I was flawed and foolish. Yes, they showed that I was no role model or saint. But they also provided a reminder of the ignorance that exists in society. They showed the hurt that can be caused by stereotyping and discrimination. They actually underlined how far we had to travel.

They also highlighted, to me at least, the importance of an apology. I have always said that I am not interested in revenge. My motive has never been to ruin careers or wreak havoc upon those who hurt me. Instead, I want an acknowledgement of what happened at Yorkshire, and I want things put in place to ensure it can't happen again. I want to be heard. An apology – a real apology that reflects genuine contrition and an understanding of error – goes a long way towards doing that. An apology should only be the start; it's the action that follows that matters.

I reflected long and hard on the generosity of spirit I'd experienced from the Jewish community, and I eventually reached out to Lord Mann to understand why my apologies had been accepted so graciously. He sent me the following explanation:

> You wanted to understand why you offended people and exactly how. People caught making offensive and derogatory comments often apologise immediately, but they do no more than that.
>
> What was interesting with you was how much you wanted to understand why you had done it and what the offence meant to a Jewish person.
>
> People rarely choose to engage with a community they have offended. You did so, but you went much further. You needed to understand how you had ended up making such offensive comments and continue to seek to understand the perspective of the Jewish community.
>
> Nobody made you spend five days on the March of the Living. You chose to do so. People who put themselves in the shoes of the Jewish person, or anyone else on the receiving end of racist abuse, are going outside their comfort zone, and this empowers the community impacted.
>
> Others could learn from what you chose to do. You were prepared to challenge your own prejudice, and I was not surprised when the Jewish community people I have spoken to warmly welcomed this.

People still come up to me and say they were disappointed by my comments. I understand that. I'm disappointed by them, too. They can never be forgotten. But I do remain deeply grateful that so many people in the Jewish community have forgiven me for them, and taken the time to educate and enlighten me. It is humbling to be treated so graciously by the people I once caused hurt to.

CHAPTER 14

Uncomfortable Conversations

I want to take a moment in this chapter to properly address my fellow South Asians. Community, which is at the heart of so much of our culture, is a powerful thing, and I believe that if we can harness that power, we will be unstoppable. But first we need to have some uncomfortable conversations about what needs to change.

Throughout this time, the moments that have stood out to me have been those when someone has told me that they are proud of what I'm doing and that they stand with me. I want to thank those people, whether you reached out to me on social media or stopped me on the street, both young and old. I am so grateful to you for motivating me when sometimes I could hardly take a shaky step.

The first event I attended after the DCMS hearing was the British Curry Awards, and a judge there came up to me, took my hand and thanked me for speaking out. She had tears in her eyes when she was addressing me. I remember holding back tears myself. I have been galvanised by these small moments of joy, and through it all they have assured me that I was doing the right thing.

However, while these experiences were important, I'm sad to say that they were few and far between. Don't get me wrong, I don't need people thanking me and congratulating me all hours of the day, but it all comes back to community, and I thought ours would be one that might be there in the hard times as well as the good. I hoped ours would rally around someone in trouble, and that we would respectfully challenge each other while working towards a common cause and goal: to fight for the equity we have been denied for so long. But it just hasn't been the case. This isn't just about my story – I see the same thing happening across our community. I don't feel we'll get the respect we deserve or the equality we have a right to until we come together. The aim of this chapter, therefore, is to serve as an uncomfortable acknowledgement of where we are and a call to action for where we need to go.

While I was going through this ordeal, I often felt lonely. While I appreciated the solidarity and support from white people, what I wanted more than anything was to feel held up by my South Asian brothers and sisters. I went to many of you for guidance, support and wisdom. I previously mentioned that I went to Hanif Malik on a number of occasions. In fact, he was one of the first people to whom I reported my concerns. As a board member at Yorkshire, awarded an OBE for his work at the Hamara Centre, a community project which undoubtedly does great work in Leeds, I felt he would understand and that it was in his interests to stand with me in my experience. At first, he was respectful and understanding. When I cried in his front room, he told me he would deal with the situation. That's why it hurt so much when I felt he wasn't supporting me.

The feeling of not being listened to by those I felt would understand the most didn't end with Hanif. I felt similarly with organisations and institutions that were specifically designed to represent South Asian and Asian cricketers. These community and faith organisations should be the voice for Asian people in the game.

Fairly early on in the proceedings, 150 Asian business owners in Yorkshire wrote a letter to the club demanding action. It was an open letter, of course, so everyone could admire their virtue. But Yorkshire responded by contacting them and inviting them to various events. Over the coming weeks, I saw photos of dozens of those involved in sending that letter posing next to significant figures from Yorkshire County Cricket Club. Some continued to sponsor the club while my situation with them was ongoing.

Nobody disappointed me more than my former teammate Ajmal Shahzad, though. Ajmal had complained about racism at Yorkshire. Tino Best, a former overseas player at the club, has made this observation, and Rana Naved-ul-Hasan has too. So, it was surprising, to put it mildly, that Ajmal should give an interview in which he said he had 'never experienced racism' in county cricket. I thought his words were damaging. This is what he said when asked about allegations of racism in county cricket: 'I knocked on five doors and none opened. I knocked on ten and none opened. So I knocked on forty-five and one of them opened. Some people might think there are barriers because they've knocked on two doors and none of them opened. But in my mind, you've not knocked on enough doors. Don't blame the person behind the door. Go knock on somebody else's door. The easy thing to say is "there's just no opportunity there" or "they look within". People get disheartened and say "it's because of this, this and this". Well, actually, no it's not, you're just not up to standard.'

For me, this promotes the idea that we must work twice as hard to get to where white people are today, and I don't believe that is right or fair. I believe in working hard, I believe in hustling and doing your bit, but I don't think we should always have to overcome these barriers to success, especially when they exist to keep us down.

I don't want this to feel like I am pointing fingers or laying blame on these individuals. While I found their actions disappointing, they speak to a wider issue in our community: people who would rather see the personal rewards and reap the benefits of assimilating than challenge the status quo, and as a wider community I feel that we allow it. Our culture instils in us the idea of not questioning our elders, not challenging their words or actions, but I think we need to start doing so to create a better future for all of us.

I realise that it's not always easy. Sport has this incredible allure that attracts people who want to bask in its reflected glow. You get to watch live matches, you are given access to the hospitality suites where you can meet people who can potentially help you to progress your career, and you're sought after and become valuable to people. But what often happens once people are brought in to drive change, particularly people of colour, is they end up stuck between a rock and a hard place. Do I say nothing, or do I put my neck on the line and take action, even though it could impact my career and my mental health, and change is probably not going to happen anyway?

I've been contacted by people on different boards in different sports to say that they are struggling to know whether to accept an invite to one event or another. I always advise them that they should go. If you've been invited to be in that room, go and be an advocate, but don't mistake your presence on its own as being indicative of progress. People often say things like, 'Look how things have changed – the room is so much more diverse.' No, there is more representation, but it's not necessarily more diverse if those people have the same perspectives and simply want to maintain the status quo. You also need diversity of thought and experience.

As a result, there are South Asians who are meant to represent us on boards, in positions of power and in politics, and many of them have backward perspectives that have gone unchallenged. We have not asked enough questions of these leaders or held them to account in furthering the causes that matter most to our community. It's not just about representation; it's about the people in power being willing to speak for the right causes. The whole cabinet in the UK could be South Asian, but if they are not supporting the marginalised or advocating for others, then there is no kinship there in my eyes. This can be seen clearly when it comes to people such as Rishi Sunak, Suella Braverman and Priti Patel.

And to be clear, there are people who represent our voice who believe 'Paki' is banter. The history of the word and the trauma it has left should make it clear that it can never be banter and should never be normalised by those in our community. The name Pakistan is made up of *Pak*, the Urdu word for 'purity', and *stan*, from the Persian word for 'place' or 'country'. Before the state of Pakistan was established in 1947, there was no ethnic group called the 'Pak' or 'Pakis', and the word 'Paki' only became widespread when it was used as a racial slur in the United Kingdom from the 1960s onwards, following a period of increased immigration to the country from South Asia. This took on an even more sinister flavour in the 1970s and '80s, when groups of skinheads and far-right sympathisers committed acts of violence against South Asians known as 'Paki-bashing'. That's why it should never be seen as acceptable.

I understand why this happens, though. People of colour are often the only ones in these spaces, so they struggle to make their voices heard. They assimilate to survive, to maintain their positions and get ahead, but when you assimilate with structures that have been set up to oppress us, you justify actions against those who look like you. People like this use the community to get into these rooms but are selfish and self-serving. They taste the power and the influence, the money and the fame, and they hoard it. I have witnessed myself that many of those with MBEs and OBEs aren't challenging the systems or representing us – they are representing their own self-interests.

People who are placed on boards or given other opportunities have a responsibility to act and need to be held to account. It's not going to work like it used to. This applies to leaders and to those from ethnic minority groups who have been brought in as advocates of change. If you become part of the system, make no bones about it, this is a different world, and we will hold you accountable. This is about our kids' futures.

That's why one of my main concerns when it comes to inclusion and diversity is fake actors – people who are using diversity to prosper or further their own interests. They don't really understand what it means or genuinely want to do things better. If you look at the websites of companies and businesses, there is inevitably a page about inclusion and their commitment to environmental, social and corporate governance, but how many are actually putting their money where their mouths are and effecting real change? You see this problem in sport and society more generally. A good example is when Yorkshire put diversity logos on their sleeves in the wake of the Black Lives Matter movement, even though the club was later shown to be institutionally racist.

For me, a lack of authenticity within this space causes more damage than good. Some individuals play the game, saying that they care about inclusion and getting rid of racism, and about mental health, but they actually sit to the side of the system and reap the benefits of saying the right things without backing up their words with actions.

A gentleman got in touch with me to say that he was joining a county that had faced similar issues to Yorkshire. He knew how bad a state the county was in, and he had lofty ambitions to change things. However, I spoke to him a few months later, and he hadn't changed anything. Instead, the institution had changed him. I'm not questioning his initial intentions, but in order to bring about change, you have to be committed and be ready to go the distance.

I cannot finish this chapter without further addressing Rishi Sunak, Suella Braverman and Priti Patel. I am frustrated and saddened that these people are or have been in the position to wield political power to enact real change. Representation does not solve all issues; it is a plaster over a deep wound, and it doesn't automatically create sustainable change.

Sadly, their behaviour seems to suggest to me that they've done what others from South Asian backgrounds sometimes do when they get into positions of power, they pull the ladder up behind themselves. It's unacceptable, prideful and egotistical to want to be the only South Asian in the room when there is enough space for all of us. I often hear people say things like, 'I'm the only one,' or, 'I'm the first one,' and although that's a good thing and something to be proud of, the more important thing is how many more people you can open the door for so that you're not the only one.

It's also fairly easy to find someone who aligns with the status quo – it's much harder to find someone willing to sacrifice everything to challenge it. Often these people do more damage than good. Sunak, Patel and Braverman continue to spread the kind of hateful rhetoric that has always been directed at their own people. Just because you are brown doesn't mean you cannot be prejudiced.

It's heartbreaking to see these politicians bring in policies that would have had a horrendous impact on them and their own families in years past. I worry about their influence on future generations. I would love to get in a room with them and ask, 'What the hell are you doing?' Maybe I'll get an invitation when this book launches – I doubt it, though!

Brown people will always be second-class citizens if we don't take risks. We need to come together to demand respect and for our contributions to wider society to be celebrated. We should take real inspiration from the Black Lives Matter civil rights movement and the black people who boldly stood up and said, 'Enough is enough', who marched together and held each other up. As I said before, seeing this movement has been such an important part of my journey, and I have learned so much from witnessing it. However, right now they face 'ally-ship fatigue', whereby advocates for their cause are becoming exhausted or tired with the uncomfortable conversations. But they are a *must*. And we all need to become more at ease with challenging and being challenged.

For South Asians, our mode of operation has not worked. If you keep doing the same things, you get the same results. There needs to be change. Let's come together for one purpose. This requires selflessness and sacrifice in the moment but could lead to great rewards for the future and for our children. Currently, we are the easiest community to divide and rule. This is a call to action to change that.

So, what are some actionable things we can do as South Asian people to support each other and shift the dial?

Call it out

No longer can we let our voices go unheard. If there is a leader, ask them what they're doing for you. If they aren't doing enough, we need to change that leader. Although we might sometimes want to cling on to the crumbs and scraps of equality that representation provides, we need to be represented fairly.

Think about advocacy for all, not just the few

Intersectionality is essential. Part of my journey has required me to speak to people who are marginalised in different ways, and I know there are certain things as a man that I need to unlearn to better support the women around me, for example, as well as fellow people of colour. There are always things to be learned from others, and we should show solidarity with those who are also working towards equality.

Vote

Make sure you, your family and friends make the effort to vote. We have the power to choose whom we support and who represents us at decision-making levels.

Donate and share resources

Let's work together to make sure we support under-represented businesses, communities and organisations, and donate to causes that matter and make a difference to our lives. We can come together and share resources and experiences to better equip those who want to be whistle-blowers and those who want to speak up. The legal advice I had was life-changing, and I want that to be available to everyone in our community.

CHAPTER 15
Family

There was a lot that was thrown at me throughout this time. We were being hounded seven days a week, and the press published all sorts of stories about me. There were lies printed, attempts to blackmail me, things made up and the changing of simple facts. I will never shy away from fronting up for the things that I've done wrong, and I have always been 100 per cent honest, but that was not, I'm afraid to say, the case with the press.

A member of the team received a call from an ex-Yorkshire and England player near the start of this process, and he said we had no chance of succeeding, because we were taking on brand Yorkshire, something he himself had tried to do without much success. Right from the outset, the *Yorkshire Post* has taken a similar line, which they may be kicking themselves about now. When I left Yorkshire, they didn't cover my statement, with one of their journalists tweeting to say that it hadn't been sent to them, which was revealing from Yorkshire's side.

The *Post*'s approach to me went through different stages – I felt that initially, they laughed at me, probably because they didn't think my voice would be heard, then when I was gaining momentum, they began to attack me. I felt they didn't give enough weight to my side of the story. Then one of their journalists had a rant on Twitter and said I had a screw loose.

This was after me sitting on TV and talking about how close I had come to taking my own life.

I spoke to the editor of the paper, James Mitchinson, after that, and he told me how he'd had conversations with his journalists and warned some of them about their conduct towards me. I then said to James that I had all the emails from the subject access request and that I was happy to share anything with him. If he was being fed one side of the story, he could then look at the real proof instead of listening to his or his writers' friends.

Lord Patel and George Dobell made the point that the paper's role in all of this has been pretty revealing at the second DCMS select committee hearing into the state of cricket on 13 December 2022. I think history will remember the people who were on the wrong side of the argument. There's nothing they can do to change that. What you saw play out was a normal person standing up to these powerful editors and publications, and the truth has always been on my side.

Nonetheless, what my family and I were put through during this time was really challenging. I'd sat on television and spoken about how close I had come to taking my own life, but I was still considered a target, and I don't think the media or the wider cricketing world left any stone unturned in their attempts to discredit me. It was very hard to deal with.

There were the incidents at our fish-and-chip shop, and the time my parents' house was circled one night by a bloke carrying what looked like a heavy chain in his hand, and the other when a bloke walked into our house in broad daylight. We were abused on the street and on social media. I firmly believe that this was all made worse by the actions of the press. They really ought to be ashamed of themselves for printing lies and stoking the fires of abuse that came our way.

After my first appearance in front of the DCMS select committee in November 2021, when the press coverage was at its height, I got to the point where I was so scared and struggling so much mentally that I thought I was being filmed, and I couldn't have a conversation with anyone without feeling paranoid. Then, I was driving home one day, when I got this overwhelming sensation that someone was sitting next to me. This sort of thing was happening more and more, which just goes to show the effect all of this was having on me mentally.

Then, in December 2021, the ECB announced that they were launching their own investigation into racism at Yorkshire County Cricket Club. The ECB is the governing body of cricket in England and Wales, with responsibility for the county game – Yorkshire being just one of its members – and the national sides. It also has a regulatory function, with the power to charge and sanction individuals and clubs for their behaviour on and off the pitch. So, the ECB announced that they were going to investigate and charge people if necessary, and then conduct a hearing, at which I would be called as a witness.

It was ironic that the institution holding Yorkshire to account was the ECB, the game's governing body. Despite the ECB having a plan in place to tackle racism since 1999, the Independent Commission for Equity in Cricket (ICEC), which was set up by the ECB in 2021 to investigate wider inequality in the game, later showed that this was not just a Yorkshire problem – this was a countrywide problem. For example, at a DCMS select committee hearing on 25 January 2022, the county chairs gave evidence, and all of the usual tropes about why they couldn't be racist were paraded out – things like, I have a black friend, so I can't be racist; black kids just want to play football, not cricket; and Asian kids just want to study.

This is why I ultimately call into question the role of the Cricket Discipline Commission (CDC), the body charged by the ECB to investigate racism at Yorkshire County Cricket Club, as a so-called independent regulator. They were supposed to be holding Yorkshire to account, but you could argue that the ECB themselves are part of the problem and need to be held to account. I feel they are guilty of gaslighting and looking the other way. The system discriminates because it is created by leaders and by individuals. That's why it's important to not just talk about and challenge the system, but also important to talk about and challenge those who created and enabled that system.

For a lot of counties and the ECB it was easier for them to keep putting it all on Yorkshire, but the reality is that this isn't just a Yorkshire problem. As we've seen with Essex recently, as we've seen with the county chairs, as we've seen with the continued behaviour of the ECB, this is a game-wide problem at the institutional level, whether that be gaslighting or the systems that are in place not working properly, or even actively discriminating in some cases.

However, at the outset, although I felt that the ECB should have stepped in a lot sooner, I was happy to help, and I travelled down to Lord's for a preliminary interview. After I'd gone through everything again in detail, I said to them, 'I've been through hell and back, so how long is this going to take? If it's going to be just like the Squire Patton Boggs investigation, I don't want to be part of it.' I didn't think I could face another long, drawn-out process. They assured me it wouldn't take as long, but that obviously didn't play out. It wasn't until March 2023 that the CDC hearing ended up taking place.

In defence of the lawyers carrying out the investigation on behalf of the CDC, this was always going to be a really tough process, but I couldn't help wonder if they were so fearful of sections of the press that at times they didn't make the best decisions.

The ECB under Tom Harrison allowed the CDC to do their job, and I wanted to give the new ECB leadership the benefit of the doubt when they came in, but in the end I felt they weren't being very transparent.

In the meantime, the attacks kept coming, and they weren't just directed at me – they were also directed at others who were on my side or who were themselves trying to implement change in the sport. I found it particularly difficult to watch the way Lord Patel was treated. He too faced abuse and threats, and I'm convinced that this was only the case because of the colour of his skin. For example, during his appearance in front of the DCMS select committee, he read out an extract from a letter he had received, which included the following line: 'Now someone has put this guy, surname Patel, in charge to sort things out. Another coon.' He then went on to say that this letter was by no means an isolated case: 'I have a bag full of that stuff. Every time the *Yorkshire Post* puts an article in, social media would happen or letters like this would happen, people calling me "public sector jobsworth", "I only got the job because I am Asian", "I am immoral" – complaints about a whole host of stuff. I can counter that with the thousands of Yorkshire people who have been supportive, but it does impact. It impacts on you personally, it impacts on your family and it impacts on the people who work with me.'

According to every report that has been published on the topic, other chairs and leaders at Yorkshire oversaw a culture of institutional racism, yet they have never been held accountable for this. But Lord Patel, a brown man who has done some amazing things in his life, has been attacked for speaking up and trying to make things better at the club. It just reveals to me how big the problem is.

For the most part, it seemed to me that the ECB weren't taking any real action. I had conversations with James Pyemont, Head of Network Engagement at the ECB, and Tom Harrison, the CEO, and they would say, 'We're going to wait for the report,' and once the report came, it was, 'We can't do anything.' It wasn't until Sajid Javid weighed in and sponsors started leaving in droves that the ECB decided to act and took Test cricket away from Yorkshire in November 2021.

However, my view is that if there is an intention to be better, then people and organisations need to be supported. When there is acceptance and a willingness to change, a little bit of hand holding can speed things along. If there had been no opportunity for Yorkshire to improve in the past, there would have been no opportunity for them to do so in the future if they had gone bankrupt, which would have simply reopened the door for Colin Graves (although that reality came to pass anyway when he retook control of the club early in 2024). That's why I advocated for Yorkshire's Test status to be restored in 2022.

It's interesting to me that no high-profile Yorkshire players, past or present, or Test cricketers, or England captains, came out to fight publicly for Yorkshire to get Test cricket back, with a view that they were going to be better. Again, it was left to me, and I was the only person who publicly said that I thought it was important that they got it back, including in an op-ed that laid out my reasoning.

I had private conversations with Tom Harrison to keep putting the organisation under pressure, because I felt like they were going to make a knee-jerk reaction that they thought was going to make them look good, but it wouldn't help Yorkshire, or the game, or the cause. Unfortunately, as it's worked out, I was probably giving Yorkshire, and the new board and leadership, too much of the benefit of the doubt. I believe their actions have shown I shouldn't have trusted them, and they have done very little to demonstrate that they care about being better. Their attitude seems to have been that institutional racism can be fixed with a few token events promoting diversity and inclusion. The funny thing is, even when they hold an event like this, they are more likely to invite people from the establishment rather than the local community. When you think about how diverse the community is around Headingley, it makes a mockery of the club's intentions that they are seemingly so unable to reach out to the people who are right on their doorstep.

In June 2022, I was invited to Lord's to watch the Test match against New Zealand as a guest of Tom Harrison. I went along because I think it's very important that I use every opportunity to get in these rooms and challenge these people and ask them questions and have the uncomfortable conversations. It was an interesting day. Some people were very, very nice and some people weren't. I had a pleasant conversation with Tom, but I came away feeling the challenges of the previous few years had taken a toll on him.

Maybe a week later, a journalist contacted me to comment on whether there had been any halal food available at the event. The reality was that when my sister and I went up to get something to eat, we couldn't find any. Someone else at the event clearly picked up on this and went to the press. I decided to plead ignorance, because I felt it was important that we tried in some way to move forward, and I didn't feel a piece like that would help anyone, even though I do think it is important to cater for everyone at these types of events.

It wasn't the first time that food had been a part of the story, because a lot was made of it in the SPB findings. I felt this just made people feel that it was not important stuff that I was raising. I want to make it clear, I only raised three allegations: bullying, racism and institutional racism. However, the investigation broke those down into smaller incidents and complaints, some of which didn't even originate from me. I thought this made them seem inconsequential and petty. It also allowed them to say that only seven of the forty-three allegations had been upheld, thereby suggesting that the majority of my claims were false. It was done this way so people would say, 'Is that really what this is all about?'

Aside from the food at Lord's, some sections of the media had a problem with me being there in the first place. After everything that had happened, it was ironic and sad that some people were so upset about me simply watching a cricket match.

During this time, I was also being invited to speak at quite a few events. Before my DCMS select committee appearance, I didn't really know what corporate speaking was, but afterwards I was approached and asked if I'd like to speak at Linklaters, the multinational law firm based out of London, along with Mark Leftly and my PR team at Powerscourt. It was a really interesting and beneficial experience. I talked about the independent investigation and what I felt was wrong with the whole process as well as everything else that had happened up to that point. It gave me such a confidence boost, and I've found that it's been a massive part of my mental health journey. Not only has it given me another platform to spread my message, it has been therapeutic too.

On the day that I was doing my first corporate-speaking event at Linklaters on 25 January 2022, the county chairs appeared before the DCMS select committee. I was absolutely disgusted by what I heard, so I told Tom Harrison that I wanted to come and speak to the ECB board, and after a bit of hesitation, a date was arranged. I arrived at Lord's with my sister and her friend, and we met with Tom in his office. He wanted to know what I was going to say. We had a bit of a disagreement when I said that participation in the game was shrinking and he said the data showed the opposite. Meeting with the board again demonstrated to me how we'd got in such a mess. Not every member was there, but some of those who were seemed petrified. There were a few executives in attendance too, but their body language seemed to indicate that they were simply going through the motions. I went through what I felt change looked like, again hoping that I was going to be heard and listened to, but sadly the reality is that I wasn't. Every time I have met with ECB leadership, I've received grandstanding apologies and people telling me I am a hero, but that's not what I am looking for.

Off the back of my talking to the ECB board at Lord's, Ron Kalifa invited me to the Arts Club to meet with him. Some people might be impressed by stuff like that, but I'm really not. I went because I wanted to have a proper conversation about what could be done to improve things. He talked about how he was trying to get the ECB to change. That didn't wash with me – if you are a respected business leader and at that time soon to be knighted, and you can't get your voice heard in the room, then you need to ask if you are adding any value. Lots of people talk a good game but their actions don't back those words up, which makes them complicit too.

Ron rang me while everything was escalating as a result of the CDC charges that had been brought against Yorkshire and seven ex-players and suggested that I take the initiative and call Michael Vaughan. My response was, 'Hold on a minute. Don't you think I've done enough? I'm happy to talk to anyone, but why is it all on me? Why don't you show some leadership?' The reality is that most of these board members just don't want to put their necks on the line. People have promised to get in touch and then nothing. Some people might be happy to accept that, but it isn't going to wash with me.

Another talk I gave was at the law firm Mishcon de Reya. After I'd finished, Sonia Campbell, a partner at the firm, came up to me and said, 'I need to support you.' I thanked her and said I didn't think I needed any more help, because I thought my part in revealing the racism in cricket had essentially come to an end, at least in a formal sense.

But she was adamant that she wanted to help, and Mark helped me to see that Sonia would bring huge support as we moved forward. She has been a total lifesaver and as it has been throughout these events, she was another person sent by Allah to help me. She also brought on board Harry Eccles-Williams, and together they have supported me pro bono and have gone above and beyond. Sonia and Harry helped me to better understand the ECB investigation, because to begin with I wasn't represented, and ultimately the ECB lawyers had the best interests of the ECB in mind. I was only a witness, so you could argue that I didn't need to be represented by lawyers, but actually it was extremely helpful because there were huge demands on my time, and I didn't always know what the best thing to do was. There were also things that I'd had to deal with earlier in the process that I hadn't necessarily agreed with or fully understood, but I'd gone along with them because I'd had no representation; for example, when the ECB charged me for the anti-Semitic tweets. As I've said, I was more than happy to be held accountable for those comments, but I was also naive as to what this meant for the ongoing

Yorkshire investigation, and it would have been wise to have had legal advice. When Sonia and Harry came on board, their support allowed me to create separation from the ECB, which I think was really important.

It was during the following weeks and months of the investigation, with the continuing media leaks and senior journalists trying to make out as though nothing serious had ever really happened, despite me having all the proof in the world, that I came to a stark realisation, and got in touch with my team and said that I wanted to push for the ECB hearing, whenever it might happen, to be held in public. From my perspective, each part of the process had been rigged against me, but the conclusions of every report and investigation had always been to accept that I had been the victim of racial harassment and bullying. But it didn't seem to matter. Some people still didn't want to accept the truth. I had no concerns that the CDC investigation would also find in my favour, but if the hearings were conducted behind closed doors, I knew things wouldn't change and people would continue to attack me and say that I was making it all up. There was no way I was going to let people come down and say whatever they wanted in private without any accountability or proper scrutiny. Instead, I wanted everything out in the open, and I wanted proper closure and my life back.

Sonia, Harry and Nick De Marco KC, who also kindly offered to represent me pro bono, went through the ECB rules and discovered that although the organisation had never before held disciplinary proceedings in public, it was possible. So that's what we pushed for.

The ECB seemed to be pretty taken aback by this request, which I found a bit surprising. I'd come to the end of my tether with everything. I'd been vindicated over and over again, but it just didn't seem to matter for a certain section of the cricket community, including some in the media. They had no interest in anything that I'd experienced or gone through. I wanted this in public because I just wanted it to be the end.

It was around this time that new ECB leadership was announced, with Richard Thompson being appointed chair in August 2022. Not long afterwards, I had a meeting with him and said, 'From my point of view, this just needs to end, because this is not why I spoke out. And the longer this carries on, the longer it's going to take for change to happen. So let's just all sit down in a room and work this out.' But for whatever reason, he wasn't able to do that. I'm sure he has his opinions on why that is. I felt it needed someone to show leadership. Bringing people together is always the hardest thing, but if he had managed to do so, it would have been a really good start to his tenure, but unfortunately it wasn't possible.

In order to establish the form and scope of the hearing process, a preliminary hearing was held in October 2022, at which it would be decided whether the proceedings would be carried out in public or not. I went along with my legal representatives, because even though I didn't need to say or do anything, I thought it was important for me to witness the process. It was the first time I'd seen top legal professionals go about their business in a formal setting, which was really interesting. Watching Nick De Marco work was inspiring, and I was left in awe of him. One of the legal representatives said that it was important to stick with the status quo and that a hearing like this should never be held in public. To my mind, it made it look like they had something to hide. Plus, the ordeal was already being played out in public for me and my family. That very week, my parents' house was attacked again when an individual was caught on CCTV defecating in their garden.

One of the legal representatives also asked why I had accepted a settlement if I wanted my story to be heard. I didn't see the two things as being related. Yorkshire accepted the entire employment tribunal claim on the basis that it was settled, so it didn't make sense for me to pursue further. I felt very strongly that a light needed to be shone on the issue of racism in cricket more generally.

Nick talked about why we felt it was important that the hearing be held in public, arguing that it would create transparency, it was what I as the main witness wanted, and there was no reason for it not to be held in public, despite there being no precedent for this; and then there was a break for lunch. When we returned, we were in for a shock. The ECB said that their main witness (i.e. me) wanted the hearing to be in public, as did one of their leading county members, and although there had never been disciplinary hearings held in public before, if there was ever a public interest in a case, it was this one. They then said that they'd therefore decided that they wanted the proceedings to be held in public too. The CDC's adjudicating panel were so taken aback by this turn of events that they asked the ECB representative to repeat themselves.

This was quite the turnaround. In the run-up to the logistics hearing, the ECB had sent me an email in which they had accused me of derailing their efforts to bring about change by requesting the main hearing be held in public. There was of course no substance to this accusation, but it highlights how far the ECB had changed their stance when they stated that they too thought the hearing should be held in public.

Regardless of what had influenced this change of heart, we left that day very happy with the outcome. I don't suppose the

CDC panel welcomed the scrutiny, but we were confident that the ECB lawyers had left them with no choice.

We had to wait about a week for the decision, which was difficult, because details of the preliminary hearing kept getting leaked to the press. I don't know where from, but it was not helpful. When it eventually arrived, the decision was in our favour, which we were of course pleased about. However, the panel did not release their reasons for their decision. When we had made our representations to the panel, we had laid out what we meant by 'public'. And while they ultimately agreed with our position, we felt as if the proceedings did not turn out to be as open as we had hoped.

Then everyone but Michael Vaughan pulled out prior to the CDC hearing in March 2023. I have to wonder if the hearings being made public had anything to do with those players' decisions to withdraw from taking part. I think it's pretty revealing that from day one, whenever there has been an opportunity to put forward their side of the story, many haven't. Whether that be at the DCMS select committee, when Martyn Moxon, Mark Arthur and Wayne Morton didn't appear, or John Blain, Richard Pyrah, Matthew Hoggard, Tim Bresnan and Andrew Gale not coming to the CDC hearing, they've chosen not to speak up. If you've got nothing to hide, why not turn up and say what you've got to say? Despite this, the cricketing public still seems to want to view them as the victims, and I just want to make it very clear that they're definitely not.

The news that the hearing would be held in public also ramped up the press, and it ramped up some of the abuse and attacks that my family and I were receiving in a continuation of the attempts to intimidate me and try to push me back. There was even a suggestion in one of the papers that the investigation was ruining England's T20 World Cup plans. I believe this was largely an attempt to try and unsettle Adil Rashid, who was one of the main witnesses for the ECB when it came to the charge against Michael Vaughan. But Allah works his ways, and not only did England win the T20 World Cup, Adil was the outstanding performer.

It was this build-up of intimidation and abuse over the previous few years that led to me and Faryal making the decision that we had no choice but to leave the UK. It was a really difficult decision to make, but what tipped the balance was that for some time I had felt like we were just waiting for something really bad to happen. Incidents outside my parents' house were happening more and more often.

Earlier that summer, I'd played in a charity game in Dorchester in Dorset, which was about a five-hour drive from home. While I was there, Faryal rang me and said, 'I think someone's been watching our house for the past few hours.' I contacted the police to tell them what was happening, but the whole way home I was petrified about what might happen. It was moments such as that one that ultimately led to us deciding to leave. This, alongside the online threats I was receiving, I just couldn't risk my family's safety any longer.

Before we left, the ICEC commission had been due to issue their report, and I wished that they had, because it might have made people back off a little bit, and things might have been different, but it kept getting delayed, which was sad. However, it was important that they did a thorough job, and, at the end of the day, they were right to wait until it was watertight, because so many people were ready to rip their findings apart.

There was a large sense of déjà vu in the decision to leave the UK and move to Pakistan in the first instance. In 2001, my father had picked up his family and left Pakistan for safety reasons, and here I was, twenty-one years later, doing the same with my family, albeit in the opposite direction.

CHAPTER 16
Reconciliation and Healing

Faryal and I left with the kids for Pakistan in November 2022. My dad had been diagnosed with the respiratory illness COPD for a while, but he was eventually cleared to fly, and he and my mum followed not long afterwards. First, they stopped over in Dubai so he could have a break and visit my sister, who had been living there for a couple of months after she felt she had no option but to leave her role at Yorkshire because they couldn't guarantee her safety. The plan was for them to then come and join us in Pakistan, but on their first day in Dubai they both got Covid, and Dad ended up in hospital. This was the start of a difficult period for Dad and his health. We are now at the point that we know Dad's getting towards the end of his life. And the move has accelerated the decline in his lungs. This is the real-time effect of racism and speaking out. It overtakes every part of your life. I will have to live with the fact that this move, which has been the direct result of speaking out, has accelerated the end of my dad's life.

My sister had to travel to South Africa to work on the Women's World Cup that was due to be held there in February 2023, so I came to Dubai to look after my dad in December and fell in love with the place. I really liked the vibe, and I received such a warm welcome from all of the people I met.

It felt like the place to be in terms of lifestyle and career opportunities.

Though I was in Dubai, I was still very much having to deal with everything back home. I was soon back in the UK when I was asked to give further evidence to the DCMS select committee alongside Jahid Ahmed, the ex-Essex player, George Dobell and Lord Patel on 13 December 2022. The committee wanted an update on what had happened since my first appearance. I felt like there was quite a bit of resistance to change in cricket. And one of the first things I would be able to tell the committee was that I had been forced out of the country. On arrival from Dubai, I had three security guards with me 24/7, which was the sad reality of my situation.

I had dinner with George the evening before he was due to give evidence, and I could see he was a little bit nervous. As a middle-aged white man, he didn't have first-hand experience of prejudice being directed towards him, and he had never had to deal with the kind of abuse and threats that I had, but once he had become associated with me and the exposure of institutional racism in the game, he'd had to install security cameras at his house, put fences up and he too had been the subject of death threats.

I arrived at Portcullis House in the morning and waited outside the committee room with Jahid, George and Mark Leftly. Jahid and George were still a little bit nervous, but I'd obviously experienced it before, so I knew what to expect. While we were waiting, there was a technology fault, so we then had to move to the old buildings. It was so cold in there – I was literally shivering, so I turned to Mark and said, 'Am I really nervous or is it freezing?' And he replied, 'It's freezing, mate!'

Lord Patel gave his evidence virtually, as he wasn't well. George appeared at the same time, and he was pretty emotional giving his testimony. He was very open about the role of the press as he saw it, and the role of some of his colleagues, which ruffled a few feathers. But the reality is that the press has a lot of power, and a responsibility to wield that power carefully. Unfortunately, large sections of the press have a lot to answer for.

I was next, and again I felt like I was pretty measured – I just told it like I saw it, as I always did. I would have loved to have gone there and said things were getting better, but, unfortunately, that wasn't what I was seeing. Jahid gave his testimony last, and it was tough to listen to someone else talk about such similar experiences to mine.

Meanwhile, the CDC hearing kept being delayed, so over the next few months I was able to use the breathing space that my family and I enjoyed in Dubai to get ready for it. In particular, feeling like I was away from the English press was helpful, and I also took a step back from social media. It was nice to be away from the constant abuse that I'd been receiving over the previous few years. I also undertook therapy during this time, which was extremely beneficial, both in terms of my personal well-being and getting mentally prepared for the hearing. The therapy combined with the distance allowed me to feel more at ease with what was happening, helping me to deal with stuff a little bit better and begin to heal.

A few days before I was due to leave for the UK, I was told that there was a chance that my lawyers wouldn't be allowed into the hearing. It felt to me like another attempt to intimidate me and push me away and stop me from going through with my testimony. I just wanted a proper end to it all so that everyone involved could move forward with their lives. I didn't want any more 'Yeah, buts'.

I also didn't want the threat of my lawyers not being able to attend to derail me, so I got in touch with my therapist and said, 'Have you got five minutes for a quick chat?' I felt like I was going to spiral. She messaged back asking if it was urgent, and I told her it could become so. Her next response was arranging to talk the following day, along with the words, 'I will hold on to the fact that you know what to do in a crisis.' That moment really struck me, and it was a bit of a turning point for me from a mentality point of view. It made me say to myself, 'You know what, someone really believes in me. Why don't I believe in myself?'

When we spoke in the morning, we talked about what the next few weeks could bring. There was a lot of uncertainty about what might unfold, but I was left with the mindset that I would have little or no control over what would happen, and it was unlikely that everything would go exactly as I wanted it to, so I had to try and accept and be at peace with what would probably be an imperfect process. That really helped me to get ready for what was to come.

In the week leading up to the CDC hearing, there were a number of attacks on Adil's character. I wondered if this may have been an attempt to stop him attending the hearing. Though with Adil being an England player they made sure to protect him.

After my house had been attacked again in the summer of 2022, the ECB and their security guy Phil Davies had been incredible. They'd moved really quickly, providing me with 24/7 protection, which carried on right up until I left the UK and when I came back on trips prior to the CDC hearing. When I returned for the hearing in March 2023, they again provided me with three security staff. I was really thankful for this support as it helped me to feel safe, which was ultimately the most important thing. However, once the hearing was over, the security provision was removed, which was to be expected, as the ECB couldn't be responsible for my safety indefinitely.

The ECB is a big organisation, and while there are some parts of it that are less effective at what they do, I think it's important to emphasise how good Phil Davies and his security department were. The company that was brought in were also incredibly professional and helpful, and they played a big part in making me feel safe, which really contributed to me getting my confidence back.

In a taxi on the way to give evidence to the CDC hearing, I received a phone call to let me know that people had tried to break into the car in my parents' garden. I didn't think it was a coincidence. Instead, it felt like another attempt to intimidate and scare me, which was something of a recurring theme around that time, hence why I had already left the country. I was therefore extremely grateful to have the security staff to protect me.

I felt as though I handled the CDC hearing pretty comfortably. It's easy when you're telling the truth. And that's all I had to do: go there and tell the truth. But I found the behaviour of some of the people who testified extremely sad and disappointing.

I was also frustrated that the hearings weren't truly public after all as members of the public weren't able to attend, and they weren't filmed or broadcast. Instead, the proceedings were reported by the press, sections of which had proved themselves to be very much against me and seemingly determined to protect the status quo. The way that ECB witness Meena Botros's testimony played out in the room and what was reported were two very different things, with the reporting suggesting he had struggled, which just wasn't the case, and amplifying the fact that he was a person of colour. Meena was calm, clear and precise. The next morning, before the hearing started, I heard someone say, 'We knew there was a problem with cricket, but just how bigoted and racist it is has been revealed by the reporting of this process.'

Matthew Hoggard arguably said some of the most overtly racist things during my time at Yorkshire, something he at first admitted to me. But after I had done my interview with Sky after George Dobell's ESPNcricinfo piece was published, I respected the fact that he'd got in touch and apologised to me directly. We'd had a number of subsequent conversations, and I thought we were on better terms. That's why I was so staggered when towards the end of the CDC investigation, he submitted a witness statement that said I'd told him I was pursuing this cause because I didn't have 'a pot to piss in', and that he did not recall using the word 'Paki'. It's scary how easily some people forget what they've said or written in the past. Him changing his tune right towards the end was one of the most disappointing things that happened, especially because I'd been very vocal about how much I appreciated him having the courage to front up and apologise when it still wasn't really a big story.

The testimony of Matthew Wood, an ex-employee of the PCA, would have been funny if it weren't quite so disturbing. He gave statements in support of two of the accused, and he contradicted himself in them both. If there had been a live audience, or the hearings had been recorded or broadcast on YouTube, his contradictions would have been there for everyone to see, but as it was, we only had the imperfect reporting of the press to go on. The highest-profile part of his testimony was when he said I had told them I would be willing to play the race card to get on a level-four coaching course. I can categorically say that this isn't true, as I was able to prove. I had emails showing that I had gone through the application and interview process just like everyone else had. I felt that had been put in at the last minute to try and intimidate me, but also to create a printable sound bite. On the day that the ex-England captain Michael Vaughan gave evidence, the headlines that evening were about what Matthew had said.

There were a couple of other disappointing witnesses and participants in the process. I felt embarrassed for Paul Lunt, Michael Vaughan's lawyer, who in the weeks leading up to the hearing had liked a tweet which said 'Hugely looking forward to what MPV's legal team will bring to the hearing. Ensuing legal actions will be very significant.' He was pulled up on that by the panel.

Another sad thing about the CDC hearing was that it became all about one person – Michael Vaughan. He was partly to blame for that. Yes, I understand that he was the biggest name, but him making jokes such as 'It's like *Question of Sport* this' made it more about him than it needed to be. That certainly worked in the favour of Yorkshire and organisations such as the PCA and ECB, because the focus moved away from them and on to individuals. That's why I think it is so important that we turn the conversation about racism back to the institutions.

I was initially naive to this, but I am left feeling that the system is such that institutions can do almost anything they want, and what they want is to do whatever it takes to move the conversation away from racism. That might work with people not fully invested in the cause, but those of us who have suffered know exactly what is happening. That's why I am so focused on putting the spotlight back on the institutions and away from individuals in order to bring about real change.

But, apart from those exceptions, I was pretty happy with how it all went. One particularly noteworthy thing to come out of the hearings was Matthew Hoggard's statement acknowledging how much the word 'Paki' was used at the club, undermining the assertions of people like Joe Root and Colin Graves, both of whom have gone on the record to say that they never heard it used by anyone at any time.

For example, in the run-up to the 2021–22 Ashes series in Australia, the ex-England Test captain and my one-time Yorkshire teammate Joe Root told an interviewer that he stood by an earlier statement that he had never witnessed racism at the club. I found that hard to accept. To begin with, you can see how uncomfortable and nervous he is when asked about it. And Matthew Hoggard and Gary Ballance had both admitted to using racist language on a regular basis. We had all grown up together at the club, and Joe and Gary had even shared a house, so it would have been hard to avoid. I felt he was skirting around the issue and I messaged him to say how disappointed I was. We swapped some messages after that, and we were due to meet a couple of times, but we never managed to catch up with each other. Bystanders like Joe could have been leaders in the space and made a real difference.

The CDC verdict was due at the end of March, but I wasn't really bothered what it would be. I didn't need Tim O'Gorman, the chairman of the committee, or his panel to decide in my favour for me to feel vindicated. I knew what the truth was, and this was very much the end for me.

That said, I wasn't particularly impressed with the work of the CDC panel. They reneged on their promise to make the hearings public. Their communication was confusing at times, and it was pretty frustrating to deal with them. It also seemed to me like the one person of colour on the panel was there just for the optics. It was disappointing that she wasn't able to do anything.

The CDC verdict was to be made public at 10 a.m. on 31 March, but the lawyers of all the interested parties would get it in advance at 7 a.m. I said to the ECB that they needed to tell everyone at the same time, because the findings would inevitably be leaked, and it wouldn't be fair. But the ECB held firm that this was the way it would be done. I know they were trying to be clearer than clear, because they too had been the subject of many accusations, including that they and I were collaborating, and the investigation and hearing was all a massive stitch-up. If anyone saw the correspondence between me, my lawyers and the ECB, there's no way anyone could think that.

In the end, the verdict was leaked, and my team and I found out what they had ruled via an Instagram post by Michael Vaughan, which was extremely frustrating. My team and the ECB lawyers had a Zoom call to talk things through, and everyone was pretty shell-shocked by the decision and how the panel had managed to get to it.

Yorkshire and Gary Ballance had already admitted to the charges brought against them prior to the hearing, which left the verdicts on the charges brought against the six remaining defendants. All bar Michael Vaughan were found to have breached ECB directive 3.3 by engaging in 'conduct which may be prejudicial to the interests of cricket or which may bring the game of cricket or any cricketer or group of cricket-ers into disrepute' by using racist language. More specifically, the panel concluded that it was proven that Andrew Gale had called me a 'Paki' and 'Rafa the Kafir'; that Tim Bresnan had referred to Asian women, including my sister, as 'fit Pakis'; that Matthew Hoggard had called me 'Rafa the Kafir' and other Asian players at the club 'Pakis', and had referred to Ismail Dawood as 'TBM', or 'token black man'; that John Blain had used racist language, including calling Asian players 'Pakis'; and that Richard Pyrah had also used the term 'fit Paki' when referring to Asian women. The charge against Michael Vaughan that claimed he had said 'There's too many of you lot, we need to have a word about that' to me, Adil Rashid, Rana Naved-ul-Hasan and Ajmal Shahzad before a T20 game against Nottinghamshire in June 2009 was not proven. There was also one charge each for Bresnan, Hoggard and Pyrah. I had been vindicated again.

I did some media interviews straight after the verdict became public, in which I said was happy that the majority of the charges had been upheld. However, I was also quick to point out that my aim had never been to bring about sanctions against individuals: 'The issue has never been about individuals but the game as a whole. Cricket needs to understand the extent of its problems and address them. Hopefully, the structures of the game can now be rebuilt and institutionalised racism ended for good. It's time to reflect, learn and implement change.'

That same day I had another hearing in front of the ECB's Safeguarding Panel about Alex Morris and the 'red wine incident' from 2006. On the morning I had given evidence to SPB, I had spoken publicly for the first time about how as a fifteen-year-old I'd had red wine poured down my throat by Morris, though I hadn't named him at this point. I had then talked about it again in front of the select committee, which generated a lot of coverage. On the day that it had taken place, Barnsley player Andrew Ivill had been in the car, and when I spoke to SPB, he messaged me to confirm that he had been the driver and knew who was involved. This hearing was the same day as the CDC verdict and I was fasting, which was already stressful enough. The ECB found that Alex Morris had acted as I'd said and in the end he was sanctioned and told that he had to do training courses if he wanted to be involved in cricket in the future.

After the ECB had initially got in touch about safeguarding around the red wine incident following my first DCMS appearance, one of the first things they did was encourage me to speak to the police, even though I didn't really want to. When I spoke to the police, I said that I was happy to share with them what happened, but I was also very clear that I didn't want to take it any further than that. Sadly, it was as bad an experience as anything I've gone through. One officer questioned some of the witnesses without having any evidence with her, which said to me that she was just ticking a box. She also gave me a hypothetical example to demonstrate the burden of proof that really stuck with me: 'If someone raped someone and then sent them a message the next day saying it shouldn't have happened, that's not enough evidence.' I felt absolutely disgusted that a police officer dealing with safeguarding issues had used that as an example. It was another example of an institution's inability to show empathy and reinforced to me how inept they are when it comes to difficult or sensitive situations.

The day of the CDC verdict was the one on which I received some of the most horrific online abuse I ever had. It didn't seem to matter that I had been vindicated. I think some of this was down to the disingenuous way that the result was reported by some sections of the press. All of the defendants had been sanctioned except Michael Vaughan, but it was presented as though I was somehow in the wrong and had lost, which only emboldened the online trolls, encouraged by the likes of Piers Morgan, who said I should come on his show and face a proper journalist. I had done nothing but speak to 'proper' journalists over the previous few years, and I had no intention of allowing Morgan to use the interest in my case to shout at me and further his own agenda.

There were conversations about appealing the CDC verdict but I was very clear that this was to be the end. Adil messaged me that day and said, 'Allah knows.' This is something that our religion teaches us: you do as much as you can, but sometimes you get to the point where you just have to leave it to Allah. He knows what really happened.

To me, pursuing this cause was never about individuals – it was about making sure the game improved. The sanctions weren't really any concern of mine. What was important to me was that I had been vindicated, and it was now time for healing and reconciliation. Certain individuals let themselves down immensely, but that was on them, and my forgiveness wasn't the point. It was also in the past. From my perspective, it was very much about trying to find a way forward and seeing how we could make things better in the future.

I'd already started this process when I'd met with Gary Ballance in the summer of 2022 where he gave me a heartfelt apology. It was really difficult, but it was good for both of us that we were able to put what had happened to one side. And it's important that this is what happens when everyone's ready. Time is a great healer, and for the sake of the game, people do need to come together. Sections of the press also need to play their part, because, ultimately, no conflict has ever been solved without dialogue. Hopefully, that's something that will happen in the future, because so far I have received only a frosty reception.

A good example of this was when I was invited to the Ashes Test match at Old Trafford in July 2023, and I went up to the press box to see George Dobell. Although I was just saying hello to a friend, that moment offered a good snapshot of where we're at as a game, as I don't think I've ever been made to feel more uncomfortable by a group of people in my life. There were a couple of exceptions – the *Guardian*'s Jonathan Liew spoke to me, and he was absolutely lovely, as were Simon Burnton from the same paper and Lizzy Ammon from the *Times*. The same couldn't be said for the rest. I've got nothing to hide. I can have a conversation with anyone, and I'm happy to have a debate, because I know the truth is on my side, so I'm not sure why they were so reluctant to speak to me.

Some of the others made me feel uncomfortable, and that goes not just for the broadcasters and journalists who were there, but also some of the ECB leadership. It was sad, because I was just there to watch the cricket. This moment also made me realise what George was having to face; it was clearly difficult for him in that environment too.

For me, it's now about how I use my platform to promote inclusivity in cricket. As we saw when the Independent Commission for Equity in Cricket (ICEC) published their report in June 2023, being the victim of racist and bullying behaviour is not just my experience – it is the experience of many people of colour in the game. The commission had a wide brief to investigate discrimination and inequality in all aspects of the game, and this is exactly what it found. It concluded that racism in cricket was widespread and normalised, and that there were high levels of dissatisfaction with the complaints procedures when it came to reporting racism in the sport. They also highlighted a lack of representation and structural barriers for people from ethnic minority backgrounds, both at the leadership level and amongst players, saying, 'The ethnicity of male and female players at professional level does not reflect the ethnicity of the adult recreational playing base, nor the wider population of England and Wales.'

As well as rebuking the ECB for their slow response to racism in the game, the ICEC also emphasised inequality in the women's game, with both a lack of prioritisation of women's cricket and outright discrimination in terms of treatment and pay. In particular, they highlighted the restricted access to kit and facilities to women of all ages at the grassroots level in particular. And they also shone a light on the elitist nature of cricket, something that is perhaps best illustrated by the dominance of privately educated players at the top levels of the sport.

I want to take this opportunity to say a big thank you to Cindy Butts and her team at the ICEC for all they've done, because I know how challenging it was for them to maintain their independence and publish the full extent of their findings. Cindy in particular has been subjected to covert racism and has had work opportunities denied to her for fronting up, and I know how much it has taken over her life. Despite what you might have read in the press, there were all sorts of pressures put on the ICEC team in anticipation of what this report might include, so for them to stay strong and deliver was extremely admirable.

I think the ECB board that set up the ICEC commission had the right intention, but although there have been a lot of grand apologies since its report was published, I'm not sure how real the ECB's response has been, and I'd rather they keep their apologies and be a bit more active elsewhere. The ICEC report was another moment of vindication for all that I had been saying, but it also showed how big the problem is.

Recently, I was invited to an event in London to mark the end of the commission's work, and there were a number of ECB people in attendance. Richard Gould gave a speech in which he made another apology, but we don't want apologies any more – we want change. It just showed me how far off the mark cricket is, and will continue to be, unless we hold leadership's feet to the fire.

The ECB have enough people of colour who will cheerlead for them, but there's no way that they get a free pass in my eyes. If they do what they have promised, I will praise and support them, but if they gaslight us, are disingenuous about their intention to bring about change, or don't listen, I will keep shouting.

People talk a lot about justice. I think the best justice anyone can have is to feel like they've been heard. And I hope all the people who spoke to the commission, who were brave enough to recount their traumatic experiences, feel that they've been heard.

CHAPTER 17

Allyship

What does it mean to be an ally?

We've all heard this word recently. Perhaps it's on the PowerPoint slide during a mandatory office course. Perhaps it's on your social media feed. Or you may have read a book about it during the summer of 2020.

I'm not sure I ever really thought about it until I was forced to do so, and that was when I first started talking about racism in cricket.

Entering into this I was naive. I wanted to believe in the good of people, in the human capacity for empathy. I hoped that in taking these steps that I would feel seen and heard by those who had wronged me and that we could have an open and honest conversation about making amends and moving forward. It is sad that instead of taking responsibility and apologising for wronging others that so many of us are quick to jump on the defensive. And we all do it; I can't say that I am perfect either. When it comes to it and your back is against the wall, it can feel most natural to fight back and to go low, but I've learned through the years that this route will often cause more harm and escalate issues. Leading with accountability and responding with forgiveness can unite us even through the worst possible situations.

In speaking out, I was faced with a harsh reality that so many people cannot separate themselves from these structural issues, and they will do whatever they can to save themselves from criticism. I saw this from people in my community, people whom I thought I could lean on but who ultimately didn't want to threaten their own positions. I lost countless friends on this journey. Friends who thought that I was doing this for money, that I was making an issue when there wasn't one, friends who stayed silent when I needed them most. I lost colleagues and acquaintances and people I had respected for years. Some who questioned my mental health challenges. There were also those I thought could have done more. Who, if they had taken a stand, might have had a really positive impact. At points I was made to feel like there was no one I could trust.

Thankfully, there were some people who really showed up for me when they absolutely didn't need to, and they did so at great personal expense. These people were allies to me during this time, and not in a way that is just social media worthy, but in a real and often difficult way. When I was overwhelmed, exhausted and depressed, these were the people who coached me through. They saw themselves the systemic problems within cricket, and they wanted to help. They came from all different backgrounds and experiences, and they used the tools they had at their disposal to support me. They were the shining light that guided me through one of the toughest periods of my life. I am so grateful they were there as without them, I don't know where I would be.

You don't just become an ally and receive a badge and the work is done. It's not one social media post, one statement or one moment. It's a way of thinking and a mindset you carry for life. It's showing solidarity with the vulnerable and it's being selfless when protecting yourself might feel like the most attractive thing to do. It's an ongoing journey to be an ally, and it isn't something you will always get right, but the important part is trying.

George definitely didn't strike me as a likely ally at first. At the time, he was the senior correspondent for ESPNcricinfo. He was a man living in and inadvertently benefitting from the system. But my friend and journalist, James Buttler, recommended him to me. And I trust James' judgement. George had admitted to me more than once that he was drawn well out of his comfort zone by this story. He'd realised with a sense of shock that his own failure to notice the issues in cricket was part of the problem. As he put it, he had been a cricket journalist for twenty years by then, sitting next to people in the press box who looked pretty much like him and had a similar background. And he hadn't noticed. George always knew that this fight was bigger than him, bigger than me, bigger than Yorkshire County Cricket Club too. That kept us both going.

It wasn't just George, I was lucky enough to have a community. It started with Ritchie who accompanied me at the meeting and kept me sane for so long. He helped to build me back up so I could advocate for myself. It also included Taha Hashim from Wisden.com who listened to me when I told him my experiences. He was attentive, considerate and he understood the importance of what I was saying. James Buttler listened and reached out to support me on the journey consistently. The DCMS select committee listened to me when I told them my story. George's wife, Caroline, is a clinical psychologist, and I was able to speak to her when my mental health really deteriorated. She gave me strategies and she gave me perspective. She also gave me sessions of hypnosis to help reduce anxiety and to process some of the trauma I had experienced. She talked with me about post-traumatic growth: the positive change that can come from experiencing a traumatic event. It was healing and it helped me keep going.

I remember going to the ECB's first officially organised *iftar* in 2022. Its significance as the first breaking of the fast in a space which has historically been a symbol of exclusivity and privilege felt huge. And it wasn't about hearing the *azan* reverberate off its walls lined with ancient paintings of old men in antiquated clothes. No, it was also that going to Lord's that night felt like an acceptance that the ECB and MCC were really trying to be more inclusive. It felt like my story had made a difference. It felt like progress. I was nervous, but in the end I was incredibly glad I went. I remember Aatif Nawaz, the comedian who hosted the event, going off script to thank me for my courage. I remember watching Moazzam Rashid, the England disability player, who spoke through a sign language interpreter. I remember meeting leg-spinner Abtaha Maqsood, who had bowled in a hijab for Birmingham Phoenix. It felt an inclusive environment and I was proud to take part. I remember glancing across the table to see my sister, Amna, and the delight I felt at sharing this moment with her. I remember going to say my prayers in the same dressing room in which I had once suffered abuse. As the call to prayer rang out in the Long Room, I felt the enormity of the progress we had made since I first spoke out. It was overwhelming.

There were these moments of joy in the allyship I found, but there were the harder moments too. Being an ally is holding people accountable, and my friends and supporters absolutely did when the anti-Semitic messages I had exchanged with a former teammate came to light. That was an important lesson to learn. Allyship shouldn't mean just blind support for someone without respectful challenge or constructive feedback. Mark Leftly at Powerscourt was one of those who helped me confront my own shortcomings and ignorance. He didn't withdraw his support, but he did tell me to learn and improve. He believed, as did so many others, that humans can learn and change for the better. This unconditional support gave me the courage to apologise and to accept with humility I was human and flawed.

Being an ally should not be performative. If you are expecting to receive congratulation or a pat on the back then you aren't doing it right! There have been many unsung heroes in my story, those people that have taken it upon themselves to do something for me without gain and without recognition.

A great example of this would be Zahid Sheikh. I had never met Zahid Sheikh before this saga started. But he became a trusted friend and, in key moments, provided just the help I needed. Zahid runs a food packaging business in Leicester. He read that first piece on ESPNcricinfo and, through his contacts, obtained my contact details. Lots of people were in contact in those days but what really differentiated Zahid from the rest was that he offered to pay for a barrister for me. At the time, he would have had no idea if he would ever get that money back. He was far more than a financier, though. In the darkest times, I knew I could rely on his advice. He would talk to me about my tea business and suggest I focus on that. When I was anxious, he would calm me. More than once, he drove from Leicester to check that I was OK. And more than once, I would stop at his place on my way down to London and we would make the rest of the trip together.

There was also Jen Robinson, my lawyer, and a formidable human rights lawyer, who offered her services to me free of charge. She knew the work would be a big undertaking, but she was willing to do so because she knew it was important and that it could make a positive impact on the sport, and hopefully wider society.

We are influenced by our environment. Actions matter. Words matter. Values matter. We internalise so much from our environment and it has a subconscious effect. Racism has affected cricket. Racism has affected me. Racism is affecting others. It is only with alliances formed to tackle this problem that we can take it on and tear it down. It's only if those in the highest positions of power in society take action and become allies that we might see the greatest changes.

I knew my biggest challenges would come once the story went quiet and that's when Sonia Campbell and Harry Eccles-Williams got me my life back and played a huge part in helping me rebuild and move on to bigger and better things.

I hope in reading this book, you will understand that I and the allies who supported me share a simple, common goal: that everyone, anyone, regardless of the colour of their skin or where they come from, should have an equal opportunity to play cricket and never suffer for their ethnicity or religion. It really is as simple as that. I hope we can all agree that this is a positive thing. Allyship is not just a buzzword on a PowerPoint slide or on social media, it's changed my life.

I've walked a lonely road at times. But, since some of these people mentioned here became involved, and more that have supported me at various moments on the journey, I've felt we walked it together.

CONCLUSION
Moving Forward

In many ways, I was an accidental whistle-blower. I didn't even know about the term until I heard Lord Patel mention it in his press conference. While I can now see the value in speaking up to expose racism and inequality, I think it is just as important, if not more so, to suggest what some of the solutions might be. Fundamentally, the starting point has got to be acceptance that cricket has a real problem when it comes to racism. If those in positions of influence cannot acknowledge this, then solutions are not enough. If they can, then we could see exciting progress in months, not years.

To be clear, I don't have one golden nugget which will solve everything. I think we've got to re-evaluate the sporting world and how it functions and whom it protects. However, I'd like to offer my thoughts on three key areas where I see progress can happen. These are education, opportunity and accountability.

I know everyone brings up education, but that's because it's important! However, currently, our education systems are not serving their purpose. We need to educate in a more dynamic way to really reach into lives and help people see perspectives and form empathy outside of themselves. We should get people into schools and cricket youth teams with different lived experiences to speak and share their stories. This will help kids feel better represented and see role models for their future, and it will hopefully teach some kids not to be biased or prejudiced to someone who is different from them. While this may not seem life-changing, I wonder what my life would have been like if those who were racist towards me were taught more about Indian and Pakistani people. I know I would have benefitted from hearing from a Jewish person about their life. Ultimately, people are fearful of having the hard conversations or making a mistake. We need to move our communities past this through an education that creates safe spaces for learning to happen, and for minds to be changed.

Secondly, the only way to make someone feel accepted is to give them an opportunity. It's ensuring we have enough opportunities available to those who might not feel the sport is accessible to them, and removing some of the financial, social and cultural obstacles so everyone can get their opportunity to have a go. Opportunity also means that we shouldn't pigeonhole people because of their background; that we need to get the best people for roles by ensuring the opportunity is accessible to the widest expanse of people possible. Ticking a box is not a solution.

Thirdly, there is accountability. The most uncomfortable and the one which often gets avoided. A real line of accountability is important to ensure progress is made and we don't make the same mistakes again and again. Accountability doesn't and shouldn't mean loss of jobs or 'cancellation'. As long as there is acceptance, responsibility taken and a will to be better, there should always be grace given to come back from mistakes. However, there also have to be lines that cannot be crossed, as well as those where if they arc crossed more than once then there must be direct and impactful action taken. Accountability will allow us to rebuild trust. Acting will mean justice is being done.

Now, I realise that these are areas of change rather than concrete steps, but in my journey and now in my consulting and speaking work I have realised there are specific things we can do that are clear and achievable. They are often about enforcing or amending legislation so it serves everyone, not just the few.

One thing I believe has had great impact on awareness and is an example of taking accountability, is the mandatory gender pay gap reporting. Now, I think the clearest next step is for businesses, companies and sports institutions to bring in ethnicity pay gap reporting before it's made mandatory, and it should be made mandatory as soon as possible. To see where we are unrepresentative or where our funding goes means we can identify new spaces to redirect it to reduce the pay gap, and to invest in initiatives that create opportunities.

Secondly, I believe we should scrap NDAs. I believe NDAs are used to silence those who have suffered, and all they do is brush issues under the carpet. I was always clear I would never sign one and I am so glad I didn't. Transparency is how organisations will rebuild trust, and NDAs are big opaque black marks on a company's record. Real action is to be open about dealings and to help victims instead of looking after the PR or the powers of the business. By doing this we would be able to rebuild our business with humans at the forefront.

Thirdly, I will be campaigning to extend the time victims can make a claim to an employment tribunal. Currently, you have three months to bring a case forward. Three months is not nearly enough time, and usually during this time you are in no fit state to think straight. This is a technicality that favours the powerful and those upholding the status quo, and it doesn't take into account that the impact of trauma can sometimes only manifest years following the events. Abuse cases especially should extend the limit from three months to six years so there is room for accountability to happen.

Another step, and one that is particularly important to me, is to tackle mental health in sport through investment and support of organisations that offer essential services. Mental health doesn't discriminate, and so we need to ensure help is easily accessible to everyone. Men account for three out of four suicides, and suicide is the biggest cause of death for men under thirty-five; we are uniquely positioned to take on the crisis and hopefully save lives.* This mental health work needs to be completely intersectional and an open conversation. For South Asians especially, there is a culture of shame around this and it is seen as taboo.† I am intent on being a driving force to change this. It has been a pleasure to become an ambassador for MQ – a mental health research charity – and they are all about ensuring organisations do more than the bare minimum when it comes to mental health. The challenges we are facing today aren't going away and it's something we must stay on top of.

The final point I want to make is the importance of leadership. The best leadership can break boundaries, set an example and encourage authenticity. When I speak to leaders and young people, I'm struck by how the world pre-Coronavirus and the world post-Coronavirus is entirely different. Boundaries are clearer, younger people are speaking up more and feeling confident in challenging toxic workplaces. They want a work-life balance and they won't just 'put up and shut up'

---

* https://www.menshealthforum.org.uk/key-data-mental-health.
† https://www.bps.org.uk/psychologist/mental-health-south-asian-communities.

like previous generations. I admire the young people of today and tomorrow because they value their welfare and challenge the status quo. I believe leadership needs to flex and shift with these new attitudes and realities because I believe you can have a commercial and progressive workforce with better boundaries. Young people are the hope in this way and I am in awe of them. I would never have had the strength to talk as clearly and honestly as they do today. If leadership doesn't adjust and see positivity here, or upskill and make themselves better, then they may be ousted or replaced, or perhaps they won't have the tools they need to build a profitable business. I want to encourage all leaders to take it upon themselves to see what difference they can make, because they have the keys to change. If they start listening to different voices and opinions, while leading with their wealth of experience and power of influence, then environments and cultures should feel the benefits.

In cricket, a shift in our leadership is essential. Changing mindsets from self-protection to openness and honesty is what we need, as well as diversity of thought on our boards. Adding a Muslim to the board is not the change that we're looking for, if that's the extent of your actions. If you bring in people of colour so you can tick some boxes, or if you want people of colour who are going to tell you what you want to hear, that is just affirming the current status quo, not adjusting it. And we're not going to stand for it any more. We've had to suffer for a very long time, and we'll continue to fight. Consistency is also important. It's about the message being clear, and everyone getting behind in totality.

Boardrooms, if left to stagnate, do not change cultures. They stay stuck in their ways. A lot of boards are made up of people who have busy lives. They may want all the kudos that comes with it, but they don't always want the responsibilities, and they don't always want to do the hard work to improve things. At Yorkshire, there was a man willing to do this. Lord Patel confronted the racists, but it seemed he stood on his own. He felt the brunt of taking his stand, and he was attacked in the same way I was. These things take their toll, and you can only keep fighting for so long. Here's a bloke who has done some of the most amazing things and who has wide-ranging experience and knowledge, but he's been attacked again and again. It was because of all Lord Patel's hard work that Yorkshire got Test cricket back. It's a sad reflection of Yorkshire cricket, and of cricket and society more generally.

I'm adamant that board members and non-exec directors should face continual accountability in these positions. These people are there to represent us and need to take responsibility and show up in their leadership. It is also important to recruit the right people with the skills to operate well in these environments. But it's not just about non-exec directors – the same is true of anyone in a position to make decisions, whether that be executives, coaches or captains. What is the diversity of representation when it comes to the chief executives in the game? Or head coaches? Or directors of cricket? Or academy directors? As I write this, my understanding is that there is only one woman out of eighteen county chief executives, and the rest are middle-aged white men. I only know of one director of cricket who is not white, and I'm pretty sure that when it comes to academy directors, there's no diversity to speak of. This needs to change.

I will say that there are good people in the game who are trying their best – there's no doubt about that. But it's not enough. Different choices need to be made, and, as is often the case, it comes down to money. The ECB recently added more cash in the pot for central contracts. That was a choice. Instead, some or all of that money could have gone into making the game more equal. You might think it was the right decision to invest in cricket at the elite level, but I think they've got it horribly wrong. But regardless of who is correct, it all comes down to deciding what your priorities are.

Going forward, I want to practise what I preach when it comes to leadership in cricket, and campaign for solutions to problems we see across sport more generally. I want to be actively involved in bettering this sport I love so much. Many people may not have loved my methods, but as long as the results speak for themselves I will continue to feel proud of what I've done.

Beyond the sport, I am proud of where I have got to with healing from the trauma I experienced. I love living in Dubai and really enjoy bringing up my kids here. I hope one day my kids can enjoy the game I loved free of abuse. Family means the world to me, and it is therefore my sincere hope that my father, who made so many sacrifices for us over the years, will be able to spend a bit more time with us. It is lucky that being in Dubai also provides me with the access and a platform to speak to some of the biggest corporations in the world.

I feel very, very fortunate. A lot of people go through their whole lives and never find a purpose, but I've found mine. I have a passion to get out of bed every day and create opportunities for people whose voices are not being heard. And I also want to create success for myself. I was told whistle-blowers never have a successful life, but I am determined to change that because I think that will send an important message that whistle-blowers can go on to bigger and better things and it's not necessarily the end, it's only the beginning.

I began this fight on my own and I will continue to fight for this cause, regardless of the help I get now and in the future. I know how close racism and abuse brought me to taking my own life, and I therefore have first-hand experience of how much it affects people. Yes, it's uncomfortable to speak about it and put yourself in the firing line, and I've been advised that my decision to speak out will affect the rest of my life, but it is vital that we don't give up now.

I know full well that influential people have made sure I have suffered as a result of my efforts, and the covert racism continues. That's fine – my message to the powers that be is: bring it on.

It's been an incredible journey, and I've learned a lot. I have to thank everyone who has supported me. It has meant more than can ever be put into words. By telling my story, I hope to make more people aware of how damaging racism is. I want you to see that I was just a young boy who loved cricket, and I didn't deserve to be abused and pushed to the brink. Despite everything that has happened to me, the pain and the heartbreak, my wish is for everyone to see the world the same way I do: with hope. I am hopeful, for the sport, for society and for myself. The future is what we make it, so let's make it better.

Acknowledgements

I want to say a huge thank you to everyone that's supported me in getting this book, and my story, out into the world.

If it wasn't for George Dobell having a conversation with my literary agent, David Luxton, this book may never have happened. George has been a huge part of this journey since day one. He has been an advocate and a supporter of me beyond anything I could have expected, and while this book has been incredibly tough for both of us at points, our friendship has never wavered.

I feel very fortunate to have had David Luxton in my corner since our first conversation. The support from him has been outstanding.

I was absolutely blown away by the team at Orion, and especially Shyam Kumar who originally commissioned the book. He gave an emotional pitch and I saw how much my story meant to him. I knew I was in safe hands.

As this book was coming into being, I was about to move countries, the case was still ongoing and the emotions of it all were very raw. When Shyam left Orion, Katie Packer took over as the publisher for the book. Katie has been a supportive, sensitive and understanding editor, and my experience creating this book with her has been incredible.

There have been delays due to me needing to take time out, and there have been vast challenges to overcome in making sure the book is as powerful and honest as it could possibly be, yet the team at Orion were always compassionate and encouraging, and I am grateful to them all for that.

I'd also like to say a big thank you to Paul Murphy, who helped me shape my story and convey my message when we needed that extra support.

I'm over the moon with the decision I made to publish with Orion. Thank you, David, George, Shyam, Katie, Paul, Arthur, Sian, Tom and the rest of the team for all of your time, input and vision to make this book the best it could be.

I don't think I could have written this book without the support of my wife, or my family as a whole. I have had to relive the most painful parts of my story and that has been incredibly difficult. There have been nights where I didn't sleep, and times I struggled to keep going, but throughout it all my wife has been my rock.

Finally, thank *you*, whoever you are, for reading my story and opening your heart to my truth. I hope it encourages you to stand up to racism and to speak out against prejudice. I hope you will help me change the world with compassion and empathy, and help others understand that underneath our differences we are all just human beings, trying to live good lives.

CREDITS

Trapeze would like to thank everyone at Orion who worked on the publication of *It's Not Banter, It's Racism*.

Agent
David Luxton

Editors
Shyam Kumar
Katie Packer

Copy-editor
Simon Fox

Proofreader
Ian Greensill

Editorial Management
Lucinda McNeile
Serena Arthur
Jane Hughes
Charlie Panayiotou
Lucy Bilton
Claire Boyle

Audio
Paul Stark
Louise Richardson
Georgina Cutler

Contracts
Dan Herron
Ellie Bowker
Oliver Chacón

Design
Nick Shah
Jessica Hart
Joanna Ridley
Helen Ewing

Photo Shoots & Image Research
Natalie Dawkins

Finance
Nick Gibson
Jasdip Nandra
Sue Baker
Tom Costello

Inventory
Jo Jacobs
Dan Stevens

Production
Claire Keep
Francesca Sironi
Katie Horrocks

Marketing
Tom Noble

Publicity
Sian Baldwin

Sales
Catherine Worsley
Victoria Laws
Esther Waters
Tolu Ayo-Ajala
Group Sales teams across Digital, Field, International and Non-Trade

Operations
Group Sales Operations team

Rights
Rebecca Folland
Tara Hiatt
Ben Fowler
Alice Cottrell
Ruth Blakemore
Marie Henckel

Azeem Rafiq is a cricketer who played for Yorkshire CCC for two stints between 2008 and 2018. In 2012 he became the first player of Asian origin to captain Yorkshire in a senior game. In September 2020, Rafiq made accusations of racism and bullying at Yorkshire and an independent report found that a number of his accusations were true. The case became a major media story in the United Kingdom. It led to resignations at the club and was the subject of investigations by the England and Wales Cricket Board (ECB) and Digital, Culture, Media and Sport Select Committee in the British parliament.